Exodus

Back to the Bible Study Guides

Genesis: A God of Purpose, A People of Promise

Judges: Ordinary People, Extraordinary God

Proverbs: The Pursuit of God's Wisdom

Daniel: Resolute Faith in a Hostile World

John: Face-to-Face with Jesus

Ephesians: Life in God's Family

Philippians: Maturing in the Christian Life

James: Living Your Faith

Revelation: The Glorified Christ

EXODUS

GOD'S PLAN,
GOD'S PEOPLE

WOODROW KROLL

CROSSWAY BOOKS
WHEATON, ILLINOIS

Exodus: God's Plan, God's People

Copyright © 2008 by Back to the Bible

Published by Crossway Books
        a publishing ministry of Good News Publishers
        1300 Crescent Street
        Wheaton, Illinois 60187

Cover photo: iStock

First printing, 2008

Printed in the United States of America

ISBN 13: 978-1-4335-0123-4
ISBN 10: 1-4335-0123-6

Unless otherwise indicated, all Scripture quotations are taken from *The Holy Bible: English Standard Version*®. Copyright © 2001 by Crossway Bibles, a publishing ministry of Good News Publishers. Used by permission. All rights reserved.

All emphases in Scripture quotations have been added by the author.

Produced with the assistance of The Livingstone Corporation (www.LivingstoneCorp.com).

Project Staff: Neil Wilson

CH		18	17	16	15	14	13	12	11	10	09	08
15	14	13	12	11	10	9	8	7	6	5	4	3	2	1

Table of Contents

How to Use This Study

Selected passages of Exodus from the ESV are printed before each day's devotional reading, so that everything you need is in one place. While we recommend reading the Scripture passage before you read the devotional, some have found it helpful to use the devotional as preparation for reading the Scripture. If you are unfamiliar with the English Standard Version (on which this series of studies is based), you might consider reading the included Bible selection, then the devotional, then the passage again from a version that is more familiar to you. This will give you an excellent biblical basis for considering the rest of the lesson.

After each devotional, there are three sections designed to help you better understand and apply the lesson's Scripture passage.

Consider It—Several questions will give you a better understanding of the Scripture passage of the day. These could be used for a small group discussion.

Express It—Suggestions for turning the insights from the lesson into prayer.

Go Deeper—Throughout this study, you will benefit from seeing how the Book of Exodus fits with the rest of the Bible. This additional section will include other passages and insights from Scripture. The Go Deeper section will also allow you to consider some of the implications of the day's passage for the central theme of the study as well as other key Scripture themes.

God Has a Plan

Things in this world have a way of looking like they are completely out-of-hand! But appearances, as convincing as they may seem, can be misleading. God remains in control even when things seem out of control. Exodus shows us that God is always working out His plan.

Read Exodus 1:1–2:10

1 These are the names of the sons of Israel who came to Egypt with Jacob, each with his household: ²Reuben, Simeon, Levi, and Judah, ³Issachar, Zebulun, and Benjamin, ⁴Dan and Naphtali, Gad and Asher. ⁵All the descendants of Jacob were seventy persons; Joseph was already in Egypt. ⁶Then Joseph died, and all his brothers and all that generation. ⁷But the people of Israel were fruitful and increased greatly; they multiplied and grew exceedingly strong, so that the land was filled with them.

Pharaoh Oppresses Israel

⁸Now there arose a new king over Egypt, who did not know Joseph. ⁹And he said to his people, "Behold, the people of Israel are too many and too mighty for us. ¹⁰Come, let us deal shrewdly with them, lest they multiply, and, if war breaks out, they join our enemies and fight against us and escape from the land." ¹¹Therefore they set taskmasters over them to afflict them with heavy burdens. They built for Pharaoh store cities, Pithom and Raamses. ¹²But the more they were oppressed, the more they multiplied and the more they spread abroad. And the Egyptians were in dread of the people of Israel. ¹³So they ruthlessly made the people of Israel work as slaves ¹⁴and made their lives bitter with hard service, in mortar and brick, and in all kinds of work in the field. In all their work they ruthlessly made them work as slaves.

¹⁵Then the king of Egypt said to the Hebrew midwives, one of whom was named Shiphrah and the other Puah, ¹⁶"When you serve as midwife to the Hebrew women and see them on the birthstool, if it is a son, you shall kill him,

---

Key Verse

Now there arose a new king over Egypt, who did not know Joseph (Ex. 1:8).

---

but if it is a daughter, she shall live." ¹⁷But the midwives feared God and did not do as the king of Egypt commanded them, but let the male children live. ¹⁸So the king of Egypt called the midwives and said to them, "Why have you done this, and let the male children live?" ¹⁹The midwives said to Pharaoh, "Because the Hebrew women are not like the Egyptian women, for they are vigorous and give birth before the midwife comes to them." ²⁰So God dealt well with the midwives. And the people multiplied and grew very strong. ²¹And because the midwives feared God, he gave them families. ²²Then Pharaoh commanded all his people, "Every son that is born to the Hebrews you shall cast into the Nile, but you shall let every daughter live."

The Birth of Moses

2 Now a man from the house of Levi went and took as his wife a Levite woman. ²The woman conceived and bore a son, and when she saw that he was a fine child, she hid him three months. ³When she could hide him no longer, she took for him a basket made of bulrushes and daubed it with bitumen and pitch. She put the child in it and placed it among the reeds by the river bank. ⁴And his sister stood at a distance to know what would be done to him. ⁵Now the daughter of Pharaoh came down to bathe at the river, while her young women walked beside the river. She saw the basket among the reeds and sent her servant woman, and she took it. ⁶When she opened it, she saw the child, and behold, the baby was crying. She took pity on him and said, "This is one of the Hebrews' children." ⁷Then his sister said to Pharaoh's daughter, "Shall I go and call you a nurse from the Hebrew women to nurse the child for you?" ⁸And Pharaoh's daughter said to her, "Go."

So the girl went and called the child's mother. ⁹And Pharaoh's daughter said to her, "Take this child away and nurse him for me, and I will give you your wages." So the woman took the child and nursed him. ¹⁰When the child grew up, she brought him to Pharaoh's daughter, and he became her son. She named him Moses, "Because," she said, "I drew him out of the water."

Go Deeper

We don't know how many boy babies died under Pharaoh's program to prevent Israel from growing as a nation (Ex. 1:22). We don't know how many were killed in and around Bethlehem under Herod's effort to eliminate the child Jesus, "born king of the Jews" (Matt. 2:2, 16–18). We do know that people have often gone to extreme and horrible lengths to derail God's plans. We also know (or ought to) that God's plans cannot be thwarted.

Psalms 1–3 contrast the lives of those who willingly cooperate with God's plan and those who don't. The principles from these psalms apply to individual lives (Ps. 1) as well as to nations, "Why do the nations rage and the peoples plot in vain?" (Ps. 2:1). The situation may be desperate and the outlook may seem hopeless, but as David put it, "Salvation belongs to the Lord; your blessing be on your people!" (Ps. 3:8). Those who live their lives in faithful acknowledgment of God's plan discover the deep truth that, "the Lord knows the way of the righteous, but the way of the wicked will perish" (Ps. 1:6). We may not know God's plan or strategy in any given situation, but we can be certain that God does have a plan, and He will accomplish it in us!

Four hundred years is a long time. The lessons of the past are easily forgotten in that many years. Thus the Book of Exodus opens with the ominous note that Joseph, the rescuer of Egypt, had been forgotten. Within a generation or two after Jacob's sons died, their descendants in Egypt had been "fruitful and increased greatly; they multiplied and grew exceedingly strong, so that the land was filled with them" (Ex. 1:7). But the Egyptians forgot Joseph and began to fear the nation growing within their borders. And the Israelites forgot a footnote from their own history. God had told their patriarch, Abram, that his descendants would suffer: "Then the LORD said to Abram, 'Know for certain that your offspring will be sojourners in a land that is not theirs and will be servants there, and they will be afflicted for four hundred years'" (Gen. 15:13). Apparently no one was keeping track of time.

God's warning to Abram included two promises: "I will bring judgment on the nation that they serve, and afterward they shall come out with great possessions" (Gen. 15:14). God would judge the abusers and reward those who had suffered. Remembering God's promises might not have made the suffering easier, but it would have given the people a clearer reason for hope. Instead, they settled into Egypt, and they might gradually have lost their identity if God had not set them apart through suffering. God had a plan.

Seti I (Sethos), who many think was the Pharaoh who "did not know Joseph" (Ex. 1:8), built magnificent structures. He built the Hall of Columns at Thebes. He built a temple at Abydos.

He also carried out extensive buildings projects in the Nile Delta region. History remembers Seti as a ruler who built impressive buildings with rich colors and striking architectural features. But these structures, which still inspire awe today, were built with the blood, sweat, and lives of countless slaves—many of them Israelites.

Seti's son, Ramesses II, not only followed him onto the throne but also inherited his father's fondness for lavish construction projects. This was a period in which a great deal of building activity took place in Egypt. The taskmasters, who were responsible to get the work done, were hard bosses. As a result, the Israelites were deprived of any personal rights and afflicted to the point that their lives were bitter.

"Viewed from eternity's perspective, how many events will we have chalked up to accidents or coincidence that will turn out actually to have been God's deft touch at accomplishing His purposes?"

These slave masters made the people's burdens even more difficult than they really had to. The reason for this is clear from some of the other actions taken by Pharaoh's officials. They didn't just want to use the Israelites as slaves; they wanted to use them up and destroy their national, tribal identity. This is why the attempt was made to impose the killing of male babies at birth. Why kill the next generation of workers? Apparently the Egyptians didn't think they would run out of slaves, but they had a deep-seated fear of the Israelites.

Moses was born during a dangerous time for Hebrew babies. Since the midwives had not cooperated with the plan to kill the Israelites' male babies at birth, Pharaoh issued a blanket order that all Egyptians were supposed to "cast into the Nile" (1:22) any Hebrew baby boy they found. Moses' parents kept his birth secret as long as possible, but by the time he was three months old, the risk was too great. So, Moses' mother decided literally to place her child in God's care. Instead of casting her son into the Nile, she set him in a floating basket on that same river, trusting God with the outcome of his voyage. God had a plan.

Viewed from eternity's perspective, how many events will we have chalked up to accidents or coincidence that will turn out actually to have been God's deft touch at accomplishing His purposes? God used the apparent coincidence of Moses' basket bobbing in the reeds, a young woman's curiosity and mothering instincts, and a sister's courageous suggestion to advance His plan. God appointed an impromptu committee of at least four women (Pharaoh's daughter, her servant girl, Miriam, and Moses' mom) to thwart Pharaoh's plan. What better place to hide God's choice for the man who would lead His people out of bondage than in the very household of those who were in charge of the bondage?

God's plans, then and now, flourish in the face of the unlikely, the doubtful and the impossible. We should never be surprised by God's ability and sovereignty, but He delights to surprise us with His creativity. Our task is never to figure out *how* God will accomplish His purposes; our task is to unswervingly trust that He will! When God had accomplished His purposes for Israel in Egypt, He set in motion an exit strategy. When the people were finally ready to trust God, they discovered He had a plan. And that plan succeeded!

Express It

When Exodus opens, Israel has been in crushing bondage for several generations. They are reaching the point of understanding that their only hope rests in God's intervention. They are beginning to cry out to God for help. As you pray today, think about what it takes for you to trust God with the "enslaving" aspects of your life. Ask God to show you areas of your life where you may still be trying to work things out on your own rather than cooperating with the plan He has in mind for you. Trust Him with those areas He shows you.

Consider It

As you read Exodus 1:1–2:10, consider these questions:

1) What vivid mind pictures does the content of this Bible book stir up?

_____

_____

2) When Joseph's generation died, what happened to the extended family they left in Egypt?

_____

_____

3) How did Pharaoh rationalize enslaving the Hebrew people in Egypt?

_____

_____

4) What happened when the Egyptians began to treat the Israelites harshly?

_____

_____

5) In what ways did the Hebrew midwives boldly defy the death order of the Pharaoh?

_____

_____

6) What do you think Pharaoh hoped to accomplish by killing Hebrew boys but allowing the daughters to live?

_____

_____

7) What are some of the unpredictable events surrounding Moses' early survival?

_____

_____

8) How have you personally discovered "God has a plan"?

_____

_____

God Molds His Man

*God uses all our experiences in life—good and bad—
to shape us into useable servants. We may not always
see the usability of difficulties or mistakes, but God can
make miracles out of messes. And He always works on
His timetable, not ours.*

Read Exodus 2:11–4:31

Exodus 2:11–3:22

Moses Flees to Midian

¹¹One day, when Moses had grown up, he went out to his people and looked on their burdens, and he saw an Egyptian beating a Hebrew, one of his people. ¹²He looked this way and that, and seeing no one, he struck down the Egyptian and hid him in the sand. ¹³When he went out the next day, behold, two Hebrews were struggling together. And he said to the man in the wrong, "Why do you strike your companion?" ¹⁴He answered, "Who made you a prince and a judge over us? Do you mean to kill me as you killed the Egyptian?" Then Moses was afraid, and thought, "Surely the thing is known." ¹⁵When Pharaoh heard of it, he sought to kill Moses. But Moses fled from Pharaoh and stayed in the land of Midian. And he sat down by a well.

¹⁶Now the priest of Midian had seven daughters, and they came and drew water and filled the troughs to water their father's flock. ¹⁷The shepherds came and drove them away, but Moses stood up and saved them, and watered their flock. ¹⁸When they came home to their father Reuel, he said, "How is it that you have come home so soon today?" ¹⁹They said, "An Egyptian delivered us out of the hand of the shepherds and even drew water for us and watered the flock." ²⁰He said to his daughters, "Then where is he? Why have you left the man? Call him, that he may eat bread." ²¹And Moses was content to dwell with the man, and he gave Moses his daughter Zipporah. ²²She gave birth to a son, and he called his name Gershom, for he said, "I have been a sojourner in a foreign land."

God Hears Israel's Groaning

²³During those many days the king of Egypt died, and the people of Israel groaned because of their slavery and cried out for help. Their cry for rescue

> # Key Verse
>
> *"Come, I will send you to Pharaoh that you may bring my people, the children of Israel, out of Egypt"* (Ex. 3:10).

from slavery came up to God. ²⁴And God heard their groaning, and God remembered his covenant with Abraham, with Isaac, and with Jacob. ²⁵God saw the people of Israel—and God knew.

The Burning Bush

3 Now Moses was keeping the flock of his father-in-law, Jethro, the priest of Midian, and he led his flock to the west side of the wilderness and came to Horeb, the mountain of God. ²And the angel of the LORD appeared to him in a flame of fire out of the midst of a bush. He looked, and behold, the bush was burning, yet it was not consumed. ³And Moses said, "I will turn aside to see this great sight, why the bush is not burned." ⁴When the LORD saw that he turned aside to see, God called to him out of the bush, "Moses, Moses!" And he said, "Here I am." ⁵Then he said, "Do not come near; take your sandals off your feet, for the place on which you are standing is holy ground." ⁶And he said, "I am the God of your father, the God of Abraham, the God of Isaac, and the God of Jacob." And Moses hid his face, for he was afraid to look at God.

⁷Then the LORD said, "I have surely seen the affliction of my people who are in Egypt and have heard their cry because of their taskmasters. I know

their sufferings, ⁸and I have come down to deliver them out of the hand of the Egyptians and to bring them up out of that land to a good and broad land, a land flowing with milk and honey, to the place of the Canaanites, the Hittites, the Amorites, the Perizzites, the Hivites, and the Jebusites. ⁹And now, behold, the cry of the people of Israel has come to me, and I have also seen the oppression with which the Egyptians oppress them. ¹⁰Come, I will send you to Pharaoh that you may bring my people, the children of Israel, out of Egypt." ¹¹But Moses said to God, "Who am I that I should go to Pharaoh and bring the children of Israel out of Egypt?" ¹²He said, "But I will be with you, and this shall be the sign for you, that I have sent you: when you have brought the people out of Egypt, you shall serve God on this mountain."

¹³Then Moses said to God, "If I come to the people of Israel and say to them, 'The God of your fathers has sent me to you,'and they ask me, 'What is his name?' what shall I say to them?" ¹⁴God said to Moses, "I AM WHO I AM." And he said, "Say this to the people of Israel, 'I AM has sent me to you.'" ¹⁵God also said to Moses, "Say this to the people of Israel, 'The Lᴏʀᴅ, the God of your fathers, the God of Abraham, the God of Isaac, and the God of Jacob, has sent me to you.' This is my name forever, and thus I am to be remembered throughout all generations. ¹⁶Go and gather the elders of Israel together and say to them, 'The Lᴏʀᴅ, the God of your fathers, the God of Abraham, of Isaac, and of Jacob, has appeared to me, saying, "I have observed you and what has been done to you in Egypt, ¹⁷and I promise that I will bring you up out of the affliction of Egypt to the land of the Canaanites, the Hittites, the Amorites, the Perizzites, the Hivites, and the Jebusites, a land flowing with milk and honey."'¹⁸And they will listen to your voice, and you and the elders of Israel shall go to the king of Egypt and say to him, 'The Lᴏʀᴅ, the God of the Hebrews, has met with us; and now, please let us go a three days' journey into the wilderness, that we may sacrifice to the Lᴏʀᴅ our God.'¹⁹But I know that the king of Egypt will not let you go unless compelled by a mighty hand. ²⁰So I will stretch out my hand and strike Egypt with all the wonders that I will do in it; after that he will let you go. ²¹And I will give this people favor in the sight of the Egyptians; and when you go, you shall not go empty, ²²but each woman shall ask of her neighbor, and any woman who lives in her house, for silver and gold jewelry, and for clothing. You shall put them on your sons and on your daughters. So you shall plunder the Egyptians."

Go Deeper

Hebrews 11:24–27 describes this period in Moses' life as permeated with faith. The fact that Moses resisted God's call isn't so much an indication of his lack of faith in God as it is a clue to Moses' profound sense of personal inadequacy. He hadn't learned the right lesson from his early failure. He had been rudely informed that his own status wouldn't take him far, but he hadn't yet learned that as long as he was serving God no door could be permanently shut against him.

(continued)

Go Deeper Continued . . .

The marks of genuine faith were present in Moses as he grew up. At some point, he willingly turned away from the privilege of being called "the son of Pharaoh's daughter" (Heb. 11:24). He did this by faith. He realized his identification with the people of God would lead to mistreatment, but he valued that identification more than the passing pleasures offered him in Egypt (Heb. 11:25). And "he considered the reproach of Christ greater wealth than the treasures of Egypt, for he was looking to the reward" (Heb. 11:26). His attitude toward and willingness to endure suffering marks Moses as someone with the mind of Christ (Phil. 2:5) long before Christ made His extended visit to earth.

Time flies. In Exodus 2:9, Moses was three months old. In the next verse, 40 years have passed. The baby "had grown up" (Ex. 2:11). Until this point in his life, Moses lived bi-culturally. He had been raised by his mother, and he had been trained in Pharaoh's court. He had benefited from the intimate instruction he received in his birth home as a child, and he was equipped with the preparation given to a child in the most honored household in Egypt. He may have had two streams of insight and information feeding into his life, but he emerged as an adult with a single identity, a son of Israel.

It was not his formal education in Pharaoh's court but his family training in Amram and Jocebed's home (6:18, 20) that made Moses think of Israel as *his people:* "He went out to his people and looked on their burdens, and he saw an Egyptian beating a Hebrew, one of his people" (2:11). That expression of ownership points to a crucial lesson Moses needed to eventually learn: the Hebrews might technically be Moses' people, but they were absolutely and ultimately God's people. Moses was able to do little for them as long as he thought of Israel as his people. But when God commissioned Moses, the terms of ownership were made very clear: "Come, I will send you to Pharaoh that you may bring *my people,* the children of Israel, out of Egypt" (3:10). It took another 40 years for Moses to recognize God's ownership.

When Moses tried to protect one of "his" people, he discovered the first of several painful lessons. In the eyes of most Hebrews,

> " *When God sends people on a mission,*
> *He equips them with what they need,*
> *even when they don't realize it.* "

even though Moses had killed an abusive Egyptian guard, he was still from Pharaoh's privileged household. Moses' assumed role as caretaker for his people was directly challenged and rejected by one of the Israelites: "Who made you a prince and a judge over us? Do you mean to kill me as you killed the Egyptian?" (2:14). Moses must have been shocked. Not only was his secret (the murder) common knowledge, but the people he thought he could somehow help were not interested. Because of his actions, Moses obviously was no longer welcome in Pharaoh's house, but he wasn't welcome among the Israelites either! He was a man without a country, so he fled to the desert of Midian.

Exodus 2:15 tells us that Moses sat down by a well in Midian. That's how his 40-year training course in desert living began. During those years he became a father, a shepherd, and a traveler who knew the Negev wilderness like the back of his hand. He probably thought his actions had messed up any opportunity to serve God, but in reality they only revealed he wasn't ready yet. He may have thought he was hiding in the desert, but in reality God was preparing him for his life's work. He herded sheep around the Negev for 40 years as training for leading a much larger flock of humans through that same wilderness for another 40 years.

God used a tendency in Moses' life to commission him for service. Whether it was an Egyptian beating a Hebrew, two Hebrews fighting, or some bullying shepherds abusing Jethro's daughters (See 2:17), Moses naturally rushed into conflicts and wasn't afraid of the heat of battle. That's where he met God, in a burning bush (See Ex. 3.)

In Exodus 3:10 God gave Moses a mission to accomplish. And Moses wasn't exactly enthusiastic. But note he didn't refer to "my" people when he talked about the children of Israel. He had already tried to use his human credentials with the Hebrews and failed. He didn't want to do that again! But God laid out the whole plan to Moses (3:16–22) including the Egyptian resistance and God's crushing it with "wonders" (3:20). Moses answered God's call with "but behold, they will not believe me or listen to my voice" (4:1). So, God patiently gave Moses three confirming signs (staff to snake, instant leprosy, and water to blood). Moses was ready for a fight, but perhaps the years on the backside of the desert secretly filled him with doubt. Moses dragged his feet. But God gently brought him back to the point of adequacy. He gave Moses what he needed to carry out his task. When God sends people on a mission, He equips them with what they need, even when they don't realize it.

When Moses arrived back in Egypt, he didn't say a word (4:30). Aaron did the talking. The people were ready. They believed that God was finally going to answer their cries for liberation. God began to implement His exit strategy. When Moses proclaimed to Pharaoh, "Let my people go," he understood he was speaking for God, whose people he had been called to lead.

Express It

As you pray, think about the ways faith is seen in your life. Pray for opportunities to live out your faith clearly before those closest to you. Ask God to help you consider the moments of failure in your life and discern the positive lessons that might be taken from those defeats.

Consider It

As you read Exodus 2:11–4:31, consider these questions:

1) How did Moses make the transition from palace dweller to shepherd tent dweller?

_____

_____

2) Why was Moses' gesture in killing the Egyptian rejected by the Hebrews?

_____

_____

3) What kinds of skills do you think Moses learned in the Negev that he couldn't learn in Pharaoh's palace?

_____

_____

4) What royal attitudes did Moses have to "unlearn" in the desert?

_____

_____

5) Exodus 2:25 says, "God saw the people of Israel—and God knew." What did God know?

_____

_____

6) What lasting impact did the burning bush experience make on Moses?

_____

_____

7) What different excuses did Moses use to put off God's call?

_____

_____

8) Which of these excuses would you be tempted to use or have you used when faced with opportunities you sense God has placed before you?

_____

_____

Irrevocable Promises, Irreversible Purposes

The best-laid plans formulated in the quiet unity of a small group of leaders are often shattered by the crushing blows of reality. Moses and Aaron had the people behind them as they made their appointment to inform Pharaoh that God wanted His people to be let go. Pharaoh wasn't impressed.

Read Exodus 5:1–6:30

Making Bricks Without Straw

5 Afterward Moses and Aaron went and said to Pharaoh, "Thus says the LORD, the God of Israel, 'Let my people go, that they may hold a feast to me in the wilderness.'" ²But Pharaoh said, "Who is the LORD, that I should obey his voice and let Israel go? I do not know the LORD, and moreover, I will not let Israel go." ³Then they said, "The God of the Hebrews has met with us. Please let us go a three days' journey into the wilderness that we may sacrifice to the LORD our God, lest he fall upon us with pestilence or with the sword." ⁴But the king of Egypt said to them, "Moses and Aaron, why do you take the people away from their work? Get back to your burdens." ⁵And Pharaoh said, "Behold, the people of the land are now many, and you make them rest from their burdens!" ⁶The same day Pharaoh commanded the taskmasters of the people and their foremen, ⁷"You shall no longer give the people straw to make bricks, as in the past; let them go and gather straw for themselves. ⁸But the number of bricks that they made in the past you shall impose on them, you shall by no means reduce it, for they are idle. Therefore they cry, 'Let us go and offer sacrifice to our God.' ⁹Let heavier work be laid on the men that they may labor at it and pay no regard to lying words."

¹⁰So the taskmasters and the foremen of the people went out and said to the people, "Thus says Pharaoh, 'I will not give you straw. ¹¹Go and get your straw yourselves wherever you can find it, but your work will not be reduced in the least.'" ¹²So the people were scattered throughout all the land of Egypt to gather stubble for straw. ¹³The taskmasters were urgent, saying, "Complete your work, your daily task each day, as when there was straw." ¹⁴And the foremen of the people of Israel, whom Pharaoh's taskmasters had set over them, were beaten and were asked, "Why have you

not done all your task of making bricks today and yesterday, as in the past?"

¹⁵Then the foremen of the people of Israel came and cried to Pharaoh, "Why do you treat your servants like this? ¹⁶No straw is given to your servants, yet they say to us, 'Make bricks!'And behold, your servants are beaten; but the fault is in your own people." ¹⁷But he said, "You are idle, you are idle; that is why you say, 'Let us go and sacrifice to the LORD.' ¹⁸Go now and work. No straw will be given you, but you must still deliver the same number of bricks." ¹⁹The foremen of the people of Israel saw that they were in trouble when they said, "You shall by no means reduce your number of bricks, your daily task each day." ²⁰They met Moses and Aaron, who were waiting for them, as they came out from Pharaoh; ²¹and they said to them, "The LORD look on you and judge, because you have made us stink in the sight of Pharaoh and his servants, and have put a sword in their hand to kill us."

²²Then Moses turned to the LORD and said, "O Lord, why have you done evil to this people? Why did you ever send me? ²³For since I came to Pharaoh to speak in your name, he has done evil to this people, and you have not delivered your people at all."

Key Verse

But Pharaoh said, "Who is the LORD, that I should obey his voice and let Israel go? I do not know the LORD, and moreover, I will not let Israel go" (Ex. 5:2).

God Promises Deliverance

6 But the L ORD said to Moses, "Now you shall see what I will do to Pharaoh; for with a strong hand he will send them out, and with a strong hand he will drive them out of his land."

²God spoke to Moses and said to him, "I am the L ORD. ³I appeared to Abraham, to Isaac, and to Jacob, as God Almighty, but by my name the L ORD I did not make myself known to them. ⁴I also established my covenant with them to give them the land of Canaan, the land in which they lived as sojourners. ⁵Moreover, I have heard the groaning of the people of Israel whom the Egyptians hold as slaves, and I have remembered my covenant. ⁶Say therefore to the people of Israel, 'I am the L ORD, and I will bring you out from under the burdens of the Egyptians, and I will deliver you from slavery to them, and I will redeem you with an outstretched arm and with great acts of judgment. ⁷I will take you to be my people, and I will be your God, and you shall know that I am the L ORD your God, who has brought you out from under the burdens of the Egyptians. ⁸I will bring you into the land that I swore to give to Abraham, to Isaac, and to Jacob. I will give it to you for a possession. I am the L ORD.'" ⁹Moses spoke thus to the people of Israel, but they did not listen to Moses, because of their broken spirit and harsh slavery.

¹⁰So the L ORD said to Moses, ¹¹"Go in, tell Pharaoh king of Egypt to let the people of Israel go out of his land." ¹²But Moses said to the L ORD, "Behold, the people of Israel have not listened to me. How then shall Pharaoh listen to me, for I am of uncircumcised lips?" ¹³But the L ORD spoke to Moses and Aaron and gave them a charge about the people of Israel and about Pharaoh king of Egypt: to bring the people of Israel out of the land of Egypt.

The Genealogy of Moses and Aaron

¹⁴These are the heads of their fathers' houses: the sons of Reuben, the firstborn of Israel: Hanoch, Pallu, Hezron, and Carmi; these are the clans of Reuben. ¹⁵The sons of Simeon: Jemuel, Jamin, Ohad, Jachin, Zohar, and Shaul, the son of a Canaanite woman; these are the clans of Simeon. ¹⁶These are the names of the sons of Levi according to their generations: Gershon, Kohath, and Merari, the years of the life of Levi being 137 years. ¹⁷The sons of Gershon: Libni and Shimei, by their clans. ¹⁸The sons of Kohath: Amram, Izhar, Hebron, and Uzziel, the years of the life of Kohath being 133 years. ¹⁹The sons of Merari: Mahli and Mushi. These are the clans of the Levites according to their generations. ²⁰Amram took as his wife Jochebed his father's sister, and she bore him Aaron and Moses, the years of the life of Amram being 137 years. ²¹The sons of Izhar: Korah, Nepheg, and Zichri. ²²The sons of Uzziel: Mishael, Elzaphan, and Sithri. ²³Aaron took as his wife Elisheba, the daughter of Amminadab and the sister of Nahshon, and she bore him Nadab, Abihu, Eleazar, and Ithamar. ²⁴The sons of Korah: Assir, Elkanah, and Abiasaph; these are the clans of the Korahites. ²⁵Eleazar, Aaron's son, took as his wife one of the daughters of Putiel, and she bore him Phinehas. These are the heads of the fathers' houses of the Levites by their clans.

²⁶These are the Aaron and Moses to whom the L ORD said: "Bring out the people of Israel from the land of Egypt by their hosts." ²⁷It was they who spoke to Pharaoh king of Egypt about bringing out the people of Israel from Egypt, this Moses and this Aaron.

²⁸On the day when the L ORD spoke to Moses in the land of Egypt, ²⁹the L ORD said to Moses, "I am the L ORD; tell Pharaoh king of Egypt all that I say to you." ³⁰But Moses said to the L ORD, "Behold, I am of uncircumcised lips. How will Pharaoh listen to me?"

Go Deeper

It is estimated there are 7,487 promises in the Bible. While some of these are specific to individuals or nations, many of them can be claimed by any believer. But why would we trust all those promises? The only way we can trust them is if we trust the character of God—the character of God never changes.

Admittedly, we don't understand all those promises. One of the main reasons, however, we don't understand all the promises of God is because His promises rely on His purposes. And He has not entirely revealed His purposes to us. For example, there's the purpose of God in His calling us to salvation. Romans 8:28 says: "We know that for those who love God all things work together for good, for those who are called according to his purpose." While that verse is a source of comfort at times, sometimes it appears to us that all things aren't working together for good. Things appear that way because we don't know the purpose of God.

There's also the purpose of God in His election (Rom. 9:10–11). Who can understand it? Furthermore, we can't fully comprehend the purpose of His will (Eph. 1:3–10). In addition, we don't understand the purpose of His wisdom (Eph. 3:7–13). We even don't fathom totally the purpose of His salvation (2 Tim. 1:8–10). Over and over again, the Bible talks about God's purpose. Yet He does not always share that purpose with us.

So, what are we left with? We are left with God's promises. Should we trust the promises of God? Absolutely. Why should you trust the irrevocable promises of God? Because the irrevocable promises of God arise out of His irreversible purpose, and that purpose will never change. Why? Because God's character will never change.

Pharaoh wasn't used to being told he had to do anything. When Aaron and Moses showed up in his throne room with God's statement (Ex. 5:1), the ruler of Egypt said *no.* He questioned God's authority and existence, asking, "Who is the Lord"? Then, after admitting he did not know the Lord, he stated flatly, "I will not let Israel go." The tone of his words indicates that he meant to say, "Even if I did know the Lord, that doesn't mean I would feel compelled to let Israel go; so, no!" Clearly, Pharaoh didn't know whom he was facing in this confrontation. He did not realize (or did not want to believe) that behind Aaron and Moses stood the presence and power of the Lord God Almighty, Maker of heaven and earth. But he would not be left in ignorance for long.

Aaron and Moses must have been stunned. They did not expect

to be dismissed this way, coming as they did under God's authority. So, they tried a little more respectful approach using the magic word *please* and telling Pharaoh they were worried about what God might do to Israel if they didn't leave Egypt. The king responded with mockery. In his eyes, these two were just helping his slaves waste time that they should have been using to work on his projects. If they had time to dream up departure plans, they surely had time to gather straw for the bricks they were making. Instead of leaving Egypt, the people of Israel suddenly found themselves worse off than they had been. And they didn't have to look far for someone to blame—Moses and Aaron.

Moses, we read in Exodus 5:22–23, turned to God in frustration. He told God, "You have not delivered your people at all" (5:23). In effect, Moses was questioning the reliability of God's promises. Moses would have been wise at least to add the word *yet* to his declaration.

But God didn't chastise Moses for his frustration; He answered with clarification: "Now you shall see what I will do to Pharaoh" (6:1). The promise of Exodus 6:1 is based on the unchanging character of God that we see in verses 2–5. The reason you and I believe the promises of God's Word is because we believe in the character of the God who made those promises. Promises are only as good as the character of the person who makes them.

The fulfilled promises we presently enjoy, based on the unchanging character of God, also point us to God's promises yet to be filled. In Exodus 6, God reviews His past faithfulness as the preamble to His promised future actions (see vv. 2–8). Examples of God's past faithfulness should be more than enough for us to exercise trust in Him for his future promises.

But while God is the Promise Maker, there are things that hinder our believing those promises. We can see them in Exodus 6:9–12. God made promises to the Israelites, but because of their situation they wouldn't believe those promises when Moses told them. If a broken spirit and harsh slavery hinder believing the promises in verse 9, surely the fear of failure does the same in verses 10–12.

These are still some of the reasons why we don't claim the promises of God. Perhaps we have given in to a broken spirit or to life's difficulties. Maybe we are afraid we'll fail if we try to claim

> **"** *God's past faithfulness should be more than enough for us to exercise trust in Him for his future promises.* **"**

God's promises. But think for a moment about the rest of the Book of Exodus. Realize how mightily God used Moses, even when Moses thought he couldn't be used. And God didn't give up on His people, even when they didn't cooperate.

When the Lord God makes promises, they are irrevocable promises. But He also has irreversible purposes, and those we don't always know. Clearly, God's exit strategy for His people involved dealing with Egypt in judgment for enslaving Israel, creating conditions for at least partial restitution, and ultimately expelling the Hebrew nation from captivity—all in a way that could be explained only as God's intervention. In Exodus 6:1, God let Moses know that the same Pharaoh who said *no* would eventually change that to an emphatic *yes* when he acknowledged that the God he had not wanted to recognize had proven Himself the Almighty.

Express It

Two of the best opportunities that prayer provides are the means to claim God's promises and to thank God for keeping His promises. Tell Him what you are counting on, and tell Him you know He'll come through for you. Review how you let God's promises permeate your prayer life and make it a point to base your requests and thanksgiving on His promises.

Consider It

As you read Exodus 5:1–6:30, consider these questions:

1) Did Pharaoh really not know God, or do you think he had a deeper problem with any challenge to his own authority?

_____

_____

2) What effects did Moses and Aaron's visit have on the people of Israel?

_____

_____

3) How does Moses' report to God after the confrontation with Pharaoh indicate his own internal struggles?

_____

_____

4) What does God remind Moses about Himself in response to Moses' doubts?

_____

_____

5) How do you identify with the "broken spirit and harsh slavery" mentioned in 6:9?

_____

_____

6) What purpose do you see in the inclusion of Moses and Aaron's genealogy in 6:14–27?

_____

_____

7) What tone do the final two verses of chapter 6 create?

_____

_____

8) In what situations do you find that you struggle to act on God's promises?

_____

_____

Plagues and Purposes

Most of life's unforgettable lessons come with pain. The deeper our ignorance or willful resistance, the more painful will be the lesson. But even the hardest pain sometimes fails to shatter a hard heart. How would you know if there was a hard heart beating inside you?

Read Exodus 7:1–10:29

Exodus 8:1–32

The Second Plague: Frogs

8 Then the LORD said to Moses, "Go in to Pharaoh and say to him, 'Thus says the LORD, "Let my people go, that they may serve me. ²But if you refuse to let them go, behold, I will plague all your country with frogs. ³The Nile shall swarm with frogs that shall come up into your house and into your bedroom and on your bed and into the houses of your servants and your people, and into your ovens and your kneading bowls. ⁴The frogs shall come up on you and on your people and on all your servants."'" ⁵And the LORD said to Moses, "Say to Aaron, 'Stretch out your hand with your staff over the rivers, over the canals and over the pools, and make frogs come up on the land of Egypt!'" ⁶So Aaron stretched out his hand over the waters of Egypt, and the frogs came up and covered the land of Egypt. ⁷But the magicians did the same by their secret arts and made frogs come up on the land of Egypt.

⁸Then Pharaoh called Moses and Aaron and said, "Plead with the LORD to take away the frogs from me and from my people, and I will let the people go to sacrifice to the LORD." ⁹Moses said to Pharaoh, "Be pleased to command me when I am to plead for you and for your servants and for your people, that the frogs be cut off from you and your houses and be left only in the Nile." ¹⁰And he said, "Tomorrow." Moses said, "Be it as you say, so that you may know that there is no one like the LORD our God. ¹¹The frogs shall go away from you and your houses and your servants and your people. They shall be left only in the Nile." ¹²So Moses and Aaron went out from Pharaoh, and Moses cried to the LORD about the frogs, as he had agreed with Pharaoh. ¹³And the LORD did according to the word of Moses. The frogs died out in the houses, the courtyards, and the fields. ¹⁴And they gathered them together in heaps, and

> # Key Verse
>
> *"But I will harden Pharaoh's heart, and though I multiply my signs and wonders in the land of Egypt, Pharaoh will not listen to you"* (Ex. 7:3–4).

the land stank. ¹⁵But when Pharaoh saw that there was a respite, he hardened his heart and would not listen to them, as the LORD had said.

The Third Plague: Gnats

¹⁶Then the LORD said to Moses, "Say to Aaron, 'Stretch out your staff and strike the dust of the earth, so that it may become gnats in all the land of Egypt.'" ¹⁷And they did so. Aaron stretched out his hand with his staff and struck the dust of the earth, and there were gnats on man and beast. All the dust of the earth became gnats in all the land of Egypt. ¹⁸The magicians tried by their secret arts to produce gnats, but they could not. So there were gnats on man and beast. ¹⁹Then the magicians said to Pharaoh, "This is the finger of God." But Pharaoh's heart was hardened, and he would not listen to them, as the LORD had said.

The Fourth Plague: Flies

²⁰Then the LORD said to Moses, "Rise up early in the morning and present yourself to Pharaoh, as he goes out to the water, and say to him, 'Thus says the LORD, "Let my people go, that they may serve me. ²¹Or else, if you will not let my people go, behold, I will send swarms of flies on you and your servants and your people, and into your houses. And the

houses of the Egyptians shall be filled with swarms of flies, and also the ground on which they stand. ²²But on that day I will set apart the land of Goshen, where my people dwell, so that no swarms of flies shall be there, that you may know that I am the LORD in the midst of the earth. ²³Thus I will put a division between my people and your people. Tomorrow this sign shall happen.""" ²⁴And the LORD did so. There came great swarms of flies into the house of Pharaoh and into his servants' houses. Throughout all the land of Egypt the land was ruined by the swarms of flies.

²⁵Then Pharaoh called Moses and Aaron and said, "Go, sacrifice to your God within the land." ²⁶But Moses said, "It would not be right to do so, for the offerings we shall sacrifice to the LORD our God are an abomination to the Egyptians. If we sacrifice offerings abominable to the Egyptians before their eyes, will they not stone us? ²⁷We must go three days' journey into the wilderness and sacrifice to the LORD our God as he tells us." ²⁸So Pharaoh said, "I will let you go to sacrifice to the LORD your God in the wilderness; only you must not go very far away. Plead for me." ²⁹Then Moses said, "Behold, I am going out from you and I will plead with the LORD that the swarms of flies may depart from Pharaoh, from his servants, and from his people, tomorrow. Only let not Pharaoh cheat again by not letting the people go to sacrifice to the LORD." ³⁰So Moses went out from Pharaoh and prayed to the LORD. ³¹And the LORD did as Moses asked, and removed the swarms of flies from Pharaoh, from his servants, and from his people; not one remained. ³²But Pharaoh hardened his heart this time also, and did not let the people go.

Go Deeper

God's participation in hardening Pharaoh's heart during the months of agony that led up to Israel's exit from Egypt sounds harsh in modern ears. The theme of hardening comes up at least 19 times in Exodus 4–14: (4:21; 7:3, 13, 14, 22; 8:15, 19, 32; 9:7, 12, 34, 35; 10:1, 20, 27; 11:10; 14:4, 8, 17). The context of the first of these references is striking. In Exodus 4:21–23, before Moses even left the wilderness for Egypt, God told him that Pharaoh would not willingly cooperate with Israel's exit. He let Moses know how the process would conclude with the death of Pharaoh's firstborn.

Half of the references to hardening place responsibility squarely with Pharaoh. Exodus 8:15, for example, describes Pharaoh's change of heart when he discovered that God relented from the plague of frogs: "Pharaoh . . . hardened his heart." As the events unfolded, it's difficult to identify how much hardening Pharaoh did on his own and how much assistance he got from God. But God's role ensured that the real character of Pharaoh came to the front. This is illustrated by the events that followed Israel's exit. When the reality sunk in that they had just sent off much of their slave workforce, the Egyptians (including Pharaoh) changed their minds. And God hardened his heart. (See 14:4–8.) God did not do to Pharaoh what wasn't already in Pharaoh's heart to do. God simply acted to make sure that His own purposes, not Pharaoh's, were accomplished through the ruler's hardened heart.

L
ike blows from a divine sledgehammer, nine plagues descended on Egypt: blood, frogs, gnats, flies, dying livestock, boils, hail, locusts, darkness. Each of these makes us shudder in revulsion. We can hardly imagine continued resistance to God's command under such duress. Yet Pharaoh remained adamant—he would not let God's people go. What began as Pharaoh hardening his heart (Ex. 8:15, 32) reached a point where he was unable to relent because God hardened his heart (10:20, 27). God did not let Pharaoh release Israel until God's purposes were accomplished. That truth makes us shudder even more than any of the plagues. Pharaoh was afflicted with a hard heart (see Go Deeper).

When we look at each of the plagues, we discover at least one specific purpose behind God's use of it to judge Egypt. We can group the plagues into three different categories.

Three of them can be characterized as *the loathsome plagues*. The people loathed what these plagues represented. The turning of the waters of the Nile to blood (7:14–25), the frogs on the land (8:1–15) and the gnats on the land (8:16–19), demonstrate God's absolute power over the sacred things of the Egyptians. He turned their gods (the ancient Egyptians deified many natural things like the Nile and their land) into gruesome and smelly decay. Although the first two plagues were mimicked by the Egyptian magicians, the magicians were powerless against the gnats. The priests were humiliated.

The second group of plagues was *the bothersome plagues*. With the plague of flies (8:20–32), the plague on the livestock (9:1–7) and the plague of boils (9:8–12), God made a miraculous distinction between His people and the Egyptians. In the original language, the word *division* used in Exodus 8:23 means "ransom." It's the word for redemption. In essence, God is saying, "I am going to ransom My people. I'm going to keep them from these plagues, but I'm not going to protect the Egyptians." God displayed His mighty power over the details of life. The Egyptian gods were no match.

The third group of three were *the natural plagues*. During these plagues, God used a series of natural disasters to convince the

> *"The longer it takes us to learn to humble ourselves before God, to recognize that He is sovereign and we are not, the more difficult the trials that occur in our lives. And all the things that we trust as replacements for God eventually disappoint us or are destroyed."*

Egyptians that it was time to let God's people go. With the plague of hail (9:13–35), the plague of locusts (10:1–20), and the plague of darkness (10:21–29), God demonstrated His power over nature even to the targeted destruction of crops. Even the great sun god, Ra, was snuffed out by God, plunging the land of Egypt into darkness while the people of Israel continued to enjoy light in the land of Goshen.

Remember, all these plagues were calculated to hit at the very heart of Egypt's religion. The Nile was at the center of Egyptian life. All the agriculture of the country took place around the Nile, and the Nile was worshiped by the Egyptians. The Pharaoh was believed to be the offspring of the gods. More than just a punishment from God, these plagues were object lessons. They were designed specifically to teach the Egyptians that there is only one God, and He is not the Pharaoh of Egypt. He is the God of heaven.

Throughout all the plagues, we hear God's command, "Let my people go," but it is preceded by "how long will you refuse to humble yourself before me?" That is the point of what God was doing here. God was looking for Pharaoh and the Egyptians simply to humble themselves before Him; then the plagues would be removed. But the longer it took them to learn this lesson, the more severe the plagues became.

We know this principle is true in our lives. The longer it takes us to learn to humble ourselves before God, to recognize that He is sovereign and we are not, the more difficult the trials that occur in our lives. And all the things that we trust as replacements for God eventually disappoint us or are destroyed. Up to this point in the experience of the Egyptians, their lives had been preserved even though they had been miserable. Death was still coming. They had repeated opportunities to submit to God. But the deadline on opportunities was coming. That's the same deadline that awaits every human being. Once death comes, it's too late to submit.

Express It

During your prayer time, ask God, as David did: "Search me, O God, and know my heart! Try me and know my thoughts! And see if there be any grievous way in me, and lead me in the way everlasting!" (Ps. 139:23–24). Give God some time to answer that prayer when you express it to Him.

Consider It

As you read Exodus 7:1–10:29, consider these questions:

1) What did God mean when he told Moses, "I have made you like God to Pharaoh" (7:1)?

_____

_____

2) In these chapters, how many times did Moses go before Pharaoh? What did those visits accomplish?

_____

_____

3) Which of the nine plagues would you find most personally repugnant? Why?

_____

_____

4) At what point do you think Pharaoh began to realize he and his people were in trouble?

_____

_____

5) How do you see the tension between Pharaoh's willful desire to maintain control of the Hebrew slaves and God's purposes in hardening Pharaoh's heart?

_____

_____

6) How did Pharaoh attempt to "bargain" with God on several occasions?

_____

_____

7) Why do you think darkness would be such a difficult plague after everything that went before it?

_____

_____

8) How do you connect with the idea of having a hard heart? During what events in your life have you operated with what you now realize was an unyielding attitude?

_____

_____

Passover Grace

At the center of God's strategy was an actual exit. The plagues reached their climax. The people left Egypt. The Passover was experienced and then celebrated. Israel began a new life, marked by a special ceremony that would forever remind them of God's grace.

Read Exodus 11:1–12:51

Exodus 12:1–51

The Passover

12 The Lord said to Moses and Aaron in the land of Egypt, ²"This month shall be for you the beginning of months. It shall be the first month of the year for you. ³Tell all the congregation of Israel that on the tenth day of this month every man shall take a lamb according to their fathers' houses, a lamb for a household. ⁴And if the household is too small for a lamb, then he and his nearest neighbor shall take according to the number of persons; according to what each can eat you shall make your count for the lamb. ⁵Your lamb shall be without blemish, a male a year old. You may take it from the sheep or from the goats, ⁶and you shall keep it until the fourteenth day of this month, when the whole assembly of the congregation of Israel shall kill their lambs at twilight.

⁷"Then they shall take some of the blood and put it on the two doorposts and the lintel of the houses in which they eat it. ⁸They shall eat the flesh that night, roasted on the fire; with unleavened bread and bitter herbs they shall eat it. ⁹Do not eat any of it raw or boiled in water, but roasted, its head with its legs and its inner parts. ¹⁰And you shall let none of it remain until the morning; anything that remains until the morning you shall burn. ¹¹In this manner you shall eat it: with your belt fastened, your sandals on your feet, and your staff in your hand. And you shall eat it in haste. It is the Lord's Passover. ¹²For I will pass through the land of Egypt that night, and I will strike all the firstborn in the land of Egypt, both man and beast; and on all the gods of Egypt I will execute judgments: I am the Lord. ¹³The blood shall be a sign for you, on the houses where you are. And when I see the blood, I will pass over you, and no plague will befall you to destroy you, when I strike the land of Egypt.

> # Key Verse
>
> *"It was a night of watching by the Lord, to bring them out of the land of Egypt; so this same night is a night of watching kept to the Lord by all the people of Israel throughout their generations"* (Ex. 12:42).

¹⁴"This day shall be for you a memorial day, and you shall keep it as a feast to the Lord; throughout your generations, as a statute forever, you shall keep it as a feast. ¹⁵Seven days you shall eat unleavened bread. On the first day you shall remove leaven out of your houses, for if anyone eats what is leavened, from the first day until the seventh day, that person shall be cut off from Israel. ¹⁶On the first day you shall hold a holy assembly, and on the seventh day a holy assembly. No work shall be done on those days. But what everyone needs to eat, that alone may be prepared by you. ¹⁷And you shall observe the Feast of Unleavened Bread, for on this very day I brought your hosts out of the land of Egypt. Therefore you shall observe this day, throughout your generations, as a statute forever. ¹⁸In the first month, from the fourteenth day of the month at evening, you shall eat unleavened bread until the twenty-first day of the month at evening. ¹⁹For seven days no leaven is to be found in your houses. If anyone eats what is leavened, that person will be cut off from the congregation of Israel, whether he is a sojourner or a native of the land. ²⁰You shall eat nothing leavened; in all your dwelling places you shall eat unleavened bread."

²¹Then Moses called all the elders of Israel and said to them, "Go and select lambs for yourselves according to your clans, and kill the Passover lamb. ²²Take a bunch of hyssop and dip it in the blood that is in the basin, and touch the lintel and the two doorposts with the blood that is in the basin. None of you shall go out of the door of his house until the morning. ²³For the Lord will pass through to strike the Egyptians, and when he sees the blood on the lintel and on the two doorposts, the Lord will pass over the door and will not allow the destroyer to enter your houses to strike you. ²⁴You shall observe this rite as a statute for you and for your sons forever. ²⁵And when you come to the land that the Lord will give you, as he has promised, you shall keep this service. ²⁶And when your children say to you, 'What do you mean by this service?' ²⁷you shall say, 'It is the sacrifice of the Lord's Passover, for he passed over the houses of the people of Israel in Egypt, when he struck the Egyptians but spared our houses.'" And the people bowed their heads and worshiped.

²⁸Then the people of Israel went and did so; as the Lord had commanded Moses and Aaron, so they did.

The Tenth Plague: Death of the Firstborn

²⁹At midnight the Lord struck down all the firstborn in the land of Egypt, from the firstborn of Pharaoh who sat on his throne to the firstborn of the captive who was in the dungeon, and all the firstborn of the livestock. ³⁰And Pharaoh rose up in the night, he and all his servants and all the Egyptians. And there was a great cry in Egypt, for there was not a house where someone was not dead. ³¹Then he summoned Moses and Aaron by night and said, "Up, go out from among my people, both you and the people of Israel; and go, serve the Lord, as you have said. ³²Take your flocks and your herds, as you have said, and be gone, and bless me also!"

The Exodus

³³The Egyptians were urgent with the people to send them out of the land in haste. For they said, "We shall all be dead." ³⁴So the people took their dough before it was leavened, their kneading bowls being bound up in their cloaks on their shoulders. ³⁵The people of Israel had also done as Moses told them, for they had asked the Egyptians for silver and gold jewelry and for clothing. ³⁶And the Lord had given the people favor in the sight of the Egyptians, so that they let them have what they asked. Thus they plundered the Egyptians.

³⁷And the people of Israel journeyed from Rameses to Succoth, about six hundred thousand men on foot, besides women and children. ³⁸A mixed multitude also went up with them, and very much livestock, both flocks and herds. ³⁹And they baked unleavened cakes of the dough that they had brought out of Egypt, for it was not leavened, because they were thrust out of Egypt and could not wait, nor had they prepared any provisions for themselves.

⁴⁰The time that the people of Israel lived in Egypt was 430 years. ⁴¹At the end of 430 years, on that very day, all the hosts of the Lord went out from the land of Egypt. ⁴²It was a night of watching by the Lord, to bring them out of the land of Egypt; so this same night is a night of watching kept to the Lord by all the people of Israel throughout their generations.

Institution of the Passover

⁴³And the Lord said to Moses and Aaron, "This is the statute of the Passover: no foreigner shall eat of it, ⁴⁴but every slave that is bought for money may eat of it after you have circumcised him. ⁴⁵No foreigner or hired servant may eat of it. ⁴⁶It shall be eaten in one house; you shall not take any of the flesh outside the house, and you shall not break any of its bones. ⁴⁷All

the congregation of Israel shall keep it. ⁴⁸If a stranger shall sojourn with you and would keep the Passover to the Lᴏʀᴅ, let all his males be circumcised. Then he may come near and keep it; he shall be as a native of the land. But no uncircumcised person shall eat of it. ⁴⁹There shall be one law for the native and for the stranger who sojourns among you."

⁵⁰All the people of Israel did just as the Lᴏʀᴅ commanded Moses and Aaron. ⁵¹And on that very day the Lᴏʀᴅ brought the people of Israel out of the land of Egypt by their hosts.

Go Deeper

The Passover is one of three great festivals of the Hebrew people. It is first mentioned in Exodus and then traced in Leviticus, Numbers, Deuteronomy, Joshua, and 2 Chronicles. It referred to the sacrifice of the lamb in Egypt when the people of Israel were still slaves. The Hebrews smeared the blood of the lamb on the doorposts as a signal to God that He should "pass over" their houses when He destroyed all the firstborn of Egypt.

Besides the perfect lamb which provided the blood and the roasted meat for the meal, another feature of the Passover celebration is the unleavened bread. Unleavened bread was used in this celebration to demonstrate that the people had absolutely no time to allow leaven to work in their bread as they ate that final Passover meal as slaves in Egypt (Ex. 12:39). They were getting out of there in a hurry. God was delivering them after

430 years, and they were anxious to go. Jesus used the Passover's unleavened bread to represent His body, given for each of us.

By the time of the New Testament, Passover seems to have become somewhat of a pilgrim festival. Large numbers of Jews would gather in Jerusalem to observe this annual celebration. It was during one of these Passovers that Jesus was crucified at Calvary. He and His disciples ate the Passover meal together on the night before His death. Like the blood of the lamb which saved the Hebrew people from destruction in Egypt, Jesus' blood redeems us from the power of sin and death.

The first nine plagues were all difficult, but none was like the tenth. The firstborn of both man and beast died throughout the land. Even the firstborn son of Pharaoh was taken in this plague. Pharaoh's firstborn was the heir to the throne and considered to be a god. The great goddess Isis, the wife and the sister of Osiris, supposedly protected children. But when it came to the final plague, there was no contest between Isis and Yahweh. The God of Israel was proven to be the great God, the God of all gods. Those who were complicit in the killing of Israel's children 80 years earlier (Ex. 1:22) discovered for themselves the unspeakable grief of losing children or grandchildren.

The real question for us today is not whether these plagues were historical. There's no question but that they were historical. Our question is, "What did they accomplish?" What can we learn from these plagues? What do these plagues show us about God, about Egypt, and about the Israelites?

First, the plagues accomplished judgment on Egypt. That was primary in God's purposes. He says in Exodus 12:12, "For I will pass through the land of Egypt that night, and I will strike all the firstborn in the land of Egypt, both man and beast; and on all the gods of Egypt I will execute judgments: I am the LORD." The purpose of the plagues was to bring judgment on people who had rejected God.

Second, these plagues showed the superiority of Yahweh to all the other gods. Yahweh (Jehovah) and Yahweh alone is God. Israel's God is the only God. As you progress through the Book of Exodus, you learn time and time again that God is superior to every other god. The LORD is superior to all the gods of Egypt. In fact, a little later on in Exodus, when Moses appeared before his father-in-law, Jethro said, "Now I know that the LORD is greater than all gods, because in this affair they dealt arrogantly with the people" (18:11).

Third, the plagues highlighted the incompetence of the Egyptian gods. These Egyptian gods were represented by the magicians and could keep up with God for a few plagues but not for long. Satan can keep up with God for a while, but Satan is not God. When the final conflict comes, the LORD is always victorious.

Fourth, the plagues showed the impotence of Pharaoh. Here was the most powerful man on the face of the earth at the time. The

> *"Haven't you noticed that protection in your own life? In the midst of the plague of disease, in the midst of the plague of immorality, in the midst of things happening around you, it sometimes seems that the Christian lives on a bit of an island. It's a space of safety right in the midst of turbulence, because God demonstrates the protection of His own people as the storm swirls around them."*

Egyptians considered him a god, the son of Horus, the grandson of the great god Amon-Ra. Yet just like everybody else his firstborn was lost in the judgment of God.

Fifth, many Egyptians finally realized that the God of Israel was indeed the true God, and that they were worshiping a collection of false gods. When Israel left Egypt, a lot of these Egyptians left with them (12:38).

Last, the Israelites learned about God's protection for His people in the midst of turbulence. Haven't you noticed that protection in your own life? In the midst of the plague of disease, in the midst of the plague of immorality, in the midst of things happening around you, it sometimes seems that the Christian lives on a bit of an island. It's a space of safety right in the midst of turbulence, because God demonstrates the protection of His own people as the storm swirls around them.

True to His nature, God provided a way for His people to remember His exit strategy from Egypt in the centuries to come. He instituted the Passover (12:43–49; see Go Deeper). We who come after Christ understand that the Passover in the Old Testament was designed by God to point to Calvary. When the angel of death passed through the land of Egypt, he passed over the homes marked by the sign of a lamb's blood. Their protection was provided not by their own merits but by the sacrifice of another. And the key here is that the lamb was not just slain, but that the blood was applied personally to the door of each home. It was the application of the blood that signaled the death angel to "pass over" that house.

Originally, the Passover had three elements. It included the perfect Passover lamb, the unleavened bread, and the bitter herbs. Later on, a roasted egg was added as well as wine. The meal is filled with the symbolism of Christ's death.

That perfect Lamb slain for the benefit of the Israelites was also chosen to point to the perfect Son of God, who was slain for you and me. The blood from that lamb had to be applied personally to publicly announce acceptance of the benefits and blessings of God's protection and the remission of sins. The Passover was a sign. It was an example of gracious redemption that pointed to the real redemption that God would provide for us in Jesus Christ. If we look at the Passover, we see the pointer. We see the signal of God's gracious nature. If we look at Calvary, we see God's ultimate gracious action toward which Passover points.

Express It

Jesus and His disciples were celebrating Passover when they ate the Last Supper and when Jesus gave His followers the elements of Communion. How do you celebrate your relationship with Jesus Christ? Is your participation in Communion a regular part of your spiritual routine? Do you give thoughtful preparation each time you share in the Lord's Supper? As you pray, express to Christ the ways you want to be intentional about your gratitude for all that He has done for you.

Consider It

As you read Exodus 11:1–12:51, consider these questions:

1) What details did God tell Moses in Exodus 11:1-3?

_____

_____

2) To whom was Moses primarily speaking in Exodus 11:4-8?

_____

_____

3) What part of the Passover instructions stand out to you (12:1-20)?

_____

_____

4) What have you learned about the parallels between the Passover and the ministry of Jesus Christ on the cross?

_____

_____

5) How did Moses describe the arrival and effects of the tenth plague?

_____

_____

6) What did the people of Israel receive as they left Egypt?

_____

_____

7) Who do you think was in the "mixed multitude" mentioned in Exodus 12:38?

_____

_____

8) How does Exodus 12:40-42 indicate the precision of God's exit strategy?

_____

_____

Signs of God's Sovereignty

People often complain that God isn't obvious enough. He doesn't openly prove Himself to us. If He put a sign in the heavens, we would all believe. But would we? If God gave us visible signs, would we trust Him? Would we obey Him? The experience of the Israelites gives us a clue about our own responses.

Read Exodus 13:1–14:31

Consecration of the Firstborn

13 The Lord said to Moses, ²"Consecrate to me all the firstborn. Whatever is the first to open the womb among the people of Israel, both of man and of beast, is mine."

The Feast of Unleavened Bread

³Then Moses said to the people, "Remember this day in which you came out from Egypt, out of the house of slavery, for by a strong hand the Lord brought you out from this place. No leavened bread shall be eaten. ⁴Today, in the month of Abib, you are going out. ⁵And when the Lord brings you into the land of the Canaanites, the Hittites, the Amorites, the Hivites, and the Jebusites, which he swore to your fathers to give you, a land flowing with milk and honey, you shall keep this service in this month. ⁶Seven days you shall eat unleavened bread, and on the seventh day there shall be a feast to the Lord. ⁷Unleavened bread shall be eaten for seven days; no leavened bread shall be seen with you, and no leaven shall be seen with you in all your territory. ⁸You shall tell your son on that day, 'It is because of what the Lord did for me when I came out of Egypt.' ⁹And it shall be to you as a sign on your hand and as a memorial between your eyes, that the law of the Lord may be in your mouth. For with a strong hand the Lord has brought you out of Egypt. ¹⁰You shall therefore keep this statute at its appointed time from year to year.

¹¹"When the Lord brings you into the land of the Canaanites, as he swore to you and your fathers, and shall give it to you, ¹²you shall set apart to the Lord all that first opens the womb. All the firstborn of your animals that are males shall be the Lord's. ¹³Every firstborn of a donkey you shall redeem with a lamb, or

> # Key Verse
>
> *"And the Lord went before them by day in a pillar of cloud to lead them along the way, and by night in a pillar of fire to give them light, that they might travel by day and by night"* (Ex. 13:21)

if you will not redeem it you shall break its neck. Every firstborn of man among your sons you shall redeem. ¹⁴And when in time to come your son asks you, 'What does this mean?' you shall say to him, 'By a strong hand the Lord brought us out of Egypt, from the house of slavery. ¹⁵For when Pharaoh stubbornly refused to let us go, the Lord killed all the firstborn in the land of Egypt, both the firstborn of man and the firstborn of animals. Therefore I sacrifice to the Lord all the males that first open the womb, but all the firstborn of my sons I redeem.' ¹⁶It shall be as a mark on your hand or frontlets between your eyes, for by a strong hand the Lord brought us out of Egypt."

Pillars of Cloud and Fire

¹⁷When Pharaoh let the people go, God did not lead them by way of the land of the Philistines, although that was near. For God said, "Lest the people change their minds when they see war and return to Egypt." ¹⁸But God led the people around by the way of the wilderness toward the Red Sea. And the people of Israel went up out of the land of Egypt equipped for battle. ¹⁹Moses

took the bones of Joseph with him, for Joseph had made the sons of Israel solemnly swear, saying, "God will surely visit you, and you shall carry up my bones with you from here." ²⁰And they moved on from Succoth and encamped at Etham, on the edge of the wilderness. ²¹And the Lᴏʀᴅ went before them by day in a pillar of cloud to lead them along the way, and by night in a pillar of fire to give them light, that they might travel by day and by night. ²²The pillar of cloud by day and the pillar of fire by night did not depart from before the people.

Crossing the Red Sea

14 Then the Lᴏʀᴅ said to Moses, ²"Tell the people of Israel to turn back and encamp in front of Pi-hahiroth, between Migdol and the sea, in front of Baal-zephon; you shall encamp facing it, by the sea. ³For Pharaoh will say of the people of Israel, 'They are wandering in the land; the wilderness has shut them in.' ⁴And I will harden Pharaoh's heart, and he will pursue them, and I will get glory over Pharaoh and all his host, and the Egyptians shall know that I am the Lᴏʀᴅ." And they did so.

⁵When the king of Egypt was told that the people had fled, the mind of Pharaoh and his servants was changed toward the people, and they said, "What is this we have done, that we have let Israel go from serving us?" ⁶So he made ready his chariot and took his army with him, ⁷and took six hundred chosen chariots and all the other chariots of Egypt with officers over all of them. ⁸And the Lᴏʀᴅ hardened the heart of Pharaoh king of Egypt, and he pursued the people of Israel while the people of Israel were going out defiantly. ⁹The Egyptians pursued them, all Pharaoh's horses and chariots and his horsemen and his army, and overtook them encamped at the sea, by Pi-hahiroth, in front of Baal-zephon.

¹⁰When Pharaoh drew near, the people of Israel lifted up their eyes, and behold, the Egyptians were marching after them, and they feared greatly. And the people of Israel cried out to the Lᴏʀᴅ. ¹¹They said to Moses, "Is it because there are no graves in Egypt that you have taken us away to die in the wilderness? What have you done to us in bringing us out of Egypt? ¹²Is not this what we said to you in Egypt: 'Leave us alone that we may serve the Egyptians'? For it would have been better for us to serve the Egyptians than to die in the wilderness." ¹³And Moses said to the people, "Fear not, stand firm, and see the salvation of the Lᴏʀᴅ, which he will work for you today. For the Egyptians whom you see today, you shall never see again. ¹⁴The Lᴏʀᴅ will fight for you, and you have only to be silent."

¹⁵The Lᴏʀᴅ said to Moses, "Why do you cry to me? Tell the people of Israel to go forward. ¹⁶Lift up your staff, and stretch out your hand over the sea and divide it, that the people of Israel may go through the sea on dry ground. ¹⁷And I will harden the hearts of the Egyptians so that they shall go in after them, and I will get glory over Pharaoh and all his host, his chariots, and his horsemen. ¹⁸And the Egyptians shall know that I am the Lᴏʀᴅ, when I have gotten glory over Pharaoh, his chariots, and his horsemen."

¹⁹Then the angel of God who was going before the host of Israel moved and went behind them, and the pillar of cloud moved from before them and stood behind them, ²⁰coming between the host of Egypt and the host of Israel. And there was the cloud and the darkness. And it lit up the night without one coming near the other all night.

²¹Then Moses stretched out his hand over the sea, and the Lᴏʀᴅ drove the sea back by a strong east wind all night and made the sea dry land, and the waters were divided. ²²And the people of Israel went into the midst of the sea on dry ground, the waters being a wall to them on their right hand and on their left. ²³The Egyptians pursued and went in

after them into the midst of the sea, all Pharaoh's horses, his chariots, and his horsemen. ²⁴And in the morning watch the LORD in the pillar of fire and of cloud looked down on the Egyptian forces and threw the Egyptian forces into a panic, ²⁵clogging their chariot wheels so that they drove heavily. And the Egyptians said, "Let us flee from before Israel, for the LORD fights for them against the Egyptians."

²⁶Then the LORD said to Moses, "Stretch out your hand over the sea, that the water may come back upon the Egyptians, upon their chariots, and upon their horsemen." ²⁷So Moses stretched out his hand over the sea, and the sea returned to its normal course when the morning appeared. And as the Egyptians fled into it, the LORD threw the Egyptians into the midst of the sea. ²⁸The waters returned and covered the chariots and the horsemen; of all the host of Pharaoh that had followed them into the sea, not one of them remained. ²⁹But the people of Israel walked on dry ground through the sea, the waters being a wall to them on their right hand and on their left.

³⁰Thus the LORD saved Israel that day from the hand of the Egyptians, and Israel saw the Egyptians dead on the seashore. ³¹Israel saw the great power that the LORD used against the Egyptians, so the people feared the LORD, and they believed in the LORD and in his servant Moses.

Go Deeper

Do you ever wish God would appear to you in a pillar of cloud and fire? It would seem to settle a lot of questions, wouldn't it? Those amazing sights would be a constant reminder of God's presence and power. Who would have any trouble living as a dynamic follower of that kind of God?

But stop for a moment and think about how effective these pillars were with the Israelites. Almost as soon as Israel saw the Egyptian army, they panicked and began to complain to Moses. Not only that, but think about all the instances of murmuring, bickering, rebelling, and idol worship that were part of the experience of the traveling Hebrews under Moses' leadership. All of that was carried out in the "shadow" of the pillars! God's presence was right there, and it didn't seem to matter!

We assume we would never ignore God if He was that obvious in our lives. But the fact is, we do that all the time. Instead of a pillar of fire or cloud, God now reveals Himself to us through His Word—the Bible. His forever and firmly fixed Word (Ps. 119:89) is a constant reminder of who God is and what He wants for us. Still, we often ignore what is the obvious presence of God in our lives. We neglect to seek God through His Word and then complain that His will is not plain enough to us. We fail to read His promises and then question where He is when difficult things happen in our lives. Today, when we fail to engage God in His Word, are we any better off than the ancient Israelites with their pillar and cloud?

Israel was on her way, marching out of Egypt. They were munching on the last of the unleavened bread as they left their houses and slave-lives behind. They had celebrated the first Passover with their bags packed and waiting by the door. And as they set out with Moses, the word was passed around that from now on they would consecrate every firstborn to God.

Right from the beginning, God insisted that His people needed to be diligent about passing down to succeeding generations the story and significance of what had happened in Egypt (Ex. 13:8, 14). But even in these passages that brought a nation into existence and stipulated that customs like Passover were "closed" in the sense that "no foreigner shall eat of it" (12:43), that was not the whole story. Outsiders were not permanently relegated to the role of foreigner: "If a stranger shall sojourn with you and would keep the Passover to the LORD" (12:48), such a person and his household could become part of God's people.

God clearly instructed His people to take a route out of Egypt that was a dead end. Instead of following the land-bridge east of the delta of the Nile and into the Negev, the shortcut to the Promised Land, God sent them south and then east, straight toward the Red Sea. We don't know how many of the Israelites knew the route they were taking, but all of them could see the physical manifestation of God's presence with them in the cloud by day and the pillar of fire by night (13:21–22). Obviously, God was protecting them. But when Israel took her eyes off the pillar of cloud and began staring at the pursuing Egyptians (14:10), fear infiltrated the camp. Instead of simply recognizing the danger and trusting in God, they became immediately consumed with the danger and filled with doubt.

There is no question the danger was real. The grieving and angry Egyptian army was on the warpath. If they had their way, Israel would pay dearly for the death of the firstborns of Egypt. God didn't want the Israelites to pretend the enemy wasn't in hot pursuit. God wanted Israel to recognize that He was just as real as the Egyptian chariots and far greater in power than their army. Did God know the people would panic? Yes. Did He have a plan? Certainly! That's why He sent them on a dead-end path. He wanted His people to remember always

*"Fear not, stand firm, and see the salvation of the L*ORD*, which he will work for you today" (14:13). One of the negative tendencies we share with those ancient Israelites is that we, too, want to 'see the salvation of the L*ORD*' without having to 'fear not' or 'stand firm.'"*

that when there was literally nowhere else to turn, God made a way for them where there seemed to be no way.

Notice the progression of events in chapter 14. God gave Moses directions for Israel's journey and told him, "The Egyptians shall know that I am the LORD" (14:4). Israel moved out, and the Egyptians followed with a huge force. Israel saw them, feared, "cried out to the LORD" (14:10), and complained to Moses. Moses responded with words that ought to be engraved somewhere for us to see every day: "Fear not, stand firm, and see the salvation of the LORD, which he will work for you today" (14:13). One of the negative tendencies we share with those ancient Israelites is that we, too, want to "see the salvation of the LORD" without having to "fear not" or "stand firm." Neither Moses nor God waited for the people to answer the challenge. Verse 15 almost seems to indicate that Moses was about to ask God "Now what?" when God told him not to waste time crying out but to go into action with his staff.

The timing in the splitting of the Red Sea is worth picturing. Moses raised his staff apparently as night was falling. The first result was "a strong east wind" (14:21) that blew all night. Imagine how the people, restless all night, reacted when they saw, as the sun rose, that there was a dry walkway between two towering walls of water leading directly through the sea! Instead of being between a rock and a hard place, the people suddenly realized God had made a way, and they surged forward. Their passage likely took all day and part of the night. The Israelites came out the other side of the mighty reed-filled sea completely dry and safe. The Egyptians followed, but once they were between the water walls, God threw them into confusion (14:24). And then God instructed Moses to release the sea from wall duty. In an instant, the waters crashed down on the Egyptian army and crushed them. The people of Israel were given an unforgettable lesson: "Israel saw the great power that the Lord used against the Egyptians, so the people feared the Lord, and they believed in the Lord and in his servant Moses" (14:31).

Express It

Make it a point to hold your Bible as you pray next time. Do you realize it is just as much a physical sign of God's presence as the pillars of cloud and fire? Thank God for His Word and all the other reminders of His faithfulness. And practice giving His Word constant attention so that you never take Him for granted.

Consider It

As you read Exodus 13:1–14:31, consider these questions:

1) How did God explain the meaning of "consecrate to me all the firstborn"?

_____

_____

2) What was God's purpose in preparing parents to answer their children's questions about the Exodus?

_____

_____

3) What did Moses take with him when he left Egypt (13:19)? Why was that significant?

_____

_____

4) What practical effects did the people experience as a result of God's visible presence in the pillars of cloud and fire (13:21–22)?

_____

_____

5) What did God tell Moses about the pursuit of the Egyptians? What did God leave out? Why?

_____

_____

6) How did the people react when they saw the Egyptian army? What was their complaint?

_____

_____

7) Israel had God's pillars to remind them of God's presence. What sounds, sights and ideas remind you of God's presence in your life? (See Go Deeper.)

_____

_____

8) What does the crossing of the Red Sea tell you about God's ability and willingness to make a way for you in "impossible" situations?

_____

_____

Lesson 7

Songs and Complaints

Have you ever wondered what we sound like in heaven? When our prayers, praise, complaints, and questions reach God, what sounds do they make? Does God ever get tired of hearing our enthusiastic songs turn into bitter laments at the drop of a hat? The people of Israel seem an awful lot like us!

Read Exodus 15:1–17:16
Exodus 16:1–17:16

Bread from Heaven

16 They set out from Elim, and all the congregation of the people of Israel came to the wilderness of Sin, which is between Elim and Sinai, on the fifteenth day of the second month after they had departed from the land of Egypt. ²And the whole congregation of the people of Israel grumbled against Moses and Aaron in the wilderness, ³and the people of Israel said to them, "Would that we had died by the hand of the LORD in the land of Egypt, when we sat by the meat pots and ate bread to the full, for you have brought us out into this wilderness to kill this whole assembly with hunger."

⁴Then the LORD said to Moses, "Behold, I am about to rain bread from heaven for you, and the people shall go out and gather a day's portion every day, that I may test them, whether they will walk in my law or not. ⁵On the sixth day, when they prepare what they bring in, it will be twice as much as they gather daily." ⁶So Moses and Aaron said to all the people of Israel, "At evening you shall know that it was the LORD who brought you out of the land of Egypt, ⁷and in the morning you shall see the glory of the LORD, because he has heard your grumbling against the LORD. For what are we, that you grumble against us?" ⁸And Moses said, "When the LORD gives you in the evening meat to eat and in the morning bread to the full, because the LORD has heard your grumbling that you grumble against him—what are we? Your grumbling is not against us but against the LORD."

⁹Then Moses said to Aaron, "Say to the whole congregation of the people of Israel, 'Come near before the LORD, for he has heard your grumbling.'" ¹⁰And as soon as Aaron spoke to the whole congregation of the people of Israel, they looked toward the wilderness, and

> # Key Verse
>
> *And he called the name of the place Massah and Meribah, because of the quarreling of the people of Israel, and because they tested the LORD by saying, "Is the LORD among us or not?"* (Ex. 17:7).

behold, the glory of the LORD appeared in the cloud. ¹¹And the LORD said to Moses, ¹²"I have heard the grumbling of the people of Israel. Say to them, 'At twilight you shall eat meat, and in the morning you shall be filled with bread. Then you shall know that I am the LORD your God.'"

¹³In the evening quail came up and covered the camp, and in the morning dew lay around the camp. ¹⁴And when the dew had gone up, there was on the face of the wilderness a fine, flake-like thing, fine as frost on the ground. ¹⁵When the people of Israel saw it, they said to one another, "What is it?" For they did not know what it was. And Moses said to them, "It is the bread that the LORD has given you to eat. ¹⁶This is what the LORD has commanded: 'Gather of it, each one of you, as much as he can eat. You shall each take an omer, according to the number of the persons that each of you has in his tent.'" ¹⁷And the people of Israel did so. They gathered, some more, some less. ¹⁸But when they measured it with an omer, whoever gathered much had nothing left over, and whoever gathered little had no lack. Each of them gathered as much as he could eat. ¹⁹And Moses said to them, "Let no one leave

any of it over till the morning." ²⁰But they did not listen to Moses. Some left part of it till the morning, and it bred worms and stank. And Moses was angry with them. ²¹Morning by morning they gathered it, each as much as he could eat; but when the sun grew hot, it melted.

²²On the sixth day they gathered twice as much bread, two omers each. And when all the leaders of the congregation came and told Moses, ²³he said to them, "This is what the Lᴏʀᴅ has commanded: 'Tomorrow is a day of solemn rest, a holy Sabbath to the Lᴏʀᴅ; bake what you will bake and boil what you will boil, and all that is left over lay aside to be kept till the morning.'" ²⁴So they laid it aside till the morning, as Moses commanded them, and it did not stink, and there were no worms in it. ²⁵Moses said, "Eat it today, for today is a Sabbath to the Lord; today you will not find it in the field. ²⁶Six days you shall gather it, but on the seventh day, which is a Sabbath, there will be none."

²⁷On the seventh day some of the people went out to gather, but they found none. ²⁸And the Lᴏʀᴅ said to Moses, "How long will you refuse to keep my commandments and my laws? ²⁹See! The Lᴏʀᴅ has given you the Sabbath; therefore on the sixth day he gives you bread for two days. Remain each of you in his place; let no one go out of his place on the seventh day." ³⁰So the people rested on the seventh day.

³¹Now the house of Israel called its name manna. It was like coriander seed, white, and the taste of it was like wafers made with honey. ³²Moses said, "This is what the Lᴏʀᴅ has commanded: 'Let an omer of it be kept throughout your generations, so that they may see the bread with which I fed you in the wilderness, when I brought you out of the land of Egypt.'" ³³And Moses said to Aaron, "Take a jar, and put an omer of manna in it, and place it before the Lᴏʀᴅ to be kept throughout your generations."

³⁴As the Lᴏʀᴅ commanded Moses, so Aaron placed it before the testimony to be kept. ³⁵The people of Israel ate the manna forty years, till they came to a habitable land. They ate the manna till they came to the border of the land of Canaan. ³⁶(An omer is the tenth part of an ephah.)

Water from the Rock

17 All the congregation of the people of Israel moved on from the wilderness of Sin by stages, according to the commandment of the Lᴏʀᴅ, and camped at Rephidim, but there was no water for the people to drink. ²Therefore the people quarreled with Moses and said, "Give us water to drink." And Moses said to them, "Why do you quarrel with me? Why do you test the Lᴏʀᴅ?" ³But the people thirsted there for water, and the people grumbled against Moses and said, "Why did you bring us up out of Egypt, to kill us and our children and our livestock with thirst?" ⁴So Moses cried to the Lᴏʀᴅ, "What shall I do with this people? They are almost ready to stone me." ⁵And the Lᴏʀᴅ said to Moses, "Pass on before the people, taking with you some of the elders of Israel, and take in your hand the staff with which you struck the Nile, and go. ⁶Behold, I will stand before you there on the rock at Horeb, and you shall strike the rock, and water shall come out of it, and the people will drink." And Moses did so, in the sight of the elders of Israel. ⁷And he called the name of the place Massah and Meribah, because of the quarreling of the people of Israel, and because they tested the Lᴏʀᴅ by saying, "Is the Lᴏʀᴅ among us or not?"

Israel Defeats Amalek

⁸Then Amalek came and fought with Israel at Rephidim. ⁹So Moses said to Joshua, "Choose for us men, and go out and fight with Amalek. Tomorrow I will stand on the top of the hill with the

staff of God in my hand." ¹⁰So Joshua did as Moses told him, and fought with Amalek, while Moses, Aaron, and Hur went up to the top of the hill. ¹¹Whenever Moses held up his hand, Israel prevailed, and whenever he lowered his hand, Amalek prevailed. ¹²But Moses' hands grew weary, so they took a stone and put it under him, and he sat on it, while Aaron and Hur held up his hands, one on one side, and the other on the other side. So his hands were steady until the going down of the sun. ¹³And Joshua overwhelmed Amalek and his people with the sword.

¹⁴Then the LORD said to Moses, "Write this as a memorial in a book and recite it in the ears of Joshua, that I will utterly blot out the memory of Amalek from under heaven." ¹⁵And Moses built an altar and called the name of it, The Lord Is My Banner, ¹⁶saying, "A hand upon the throne of the LORD! The LORD will have war with Amalek from generation to generation."

Go Deeper

Several names or titles for God are mentioned in this lesson's passage. In Exodus 15:26, the Lord claims the title of "healer" of His people. But earlier in the song of Israel, God is declared "my strength and my song" and "my salvation" (15:2). "The LORD is a man of war" (15:3), which means He is a warrior-God who can defend those He chooses to defend and defeat those He chooses to defeat. God is also the incomparable One (15:11). In chapter 16, God is the One who hears; when we grumble against His faithful servants, we grumble against Him.

But perhaps the most striking title for God in these chapters comes in chapter 17: "And Moses built an altar and called

the name of it, The LORD is my banner" (17:15). This is the name Jehovah Nissi, expressed in Psalm 60:4. Israel had just won a great battle. Moses didn't want there to be any confusion over whose victory it really was—the Lord's. They marched under His standard, representing Him in the world.

How conscious are you of God's presence as you move through each day? We expect God's intervention when we meet difficulties, but do we think of Him as our banner during each moment of life?

The names of places (Marah, Elim, Wilderness of Sin, Rephidim, Massah and Meribah) give us the itinerary of a troubled people. Chapter 15 begins with a triumphant song of praise for God's mighty acts in breaking the bonds of slavery and setting Israel free from Egypt. Rejoicing over God's incomparable greatness echoed across the wilderness: "Who is like you, O LORD, among the gods? Who is like you majestic in holiness, awesome in glorious deeds, doing wonders?" (Ex. 15:11). As the people stood on the eastern shore of the Red Sea, looking at the wreckage of the dead Egyptian army wash up on shore, the future looked bright. They were confident. God really was guiding and protecting them.

But as soon as they turned away from the sea and stepped into the wilderness, their attitudes shifted with the sands. When they did not find fresh water and the days began to pass, they started to wonder and their faith began to wane. Then the water at Marah seemed to mock them, for it was too bitter to drink. So they cried to Moses and he cried to God. And God provided a way to sweeten the water. God also reminded them that their willingness to trust and obey Him would keep them from experiencing the same kind of consequences that the Egyptians suffered. He gave them a new title to use for Him: "I am the LORD, your healer" (15:26).

Their next stop was Elim, with abundant water and palm trees, a striking contrast to Marah. God gave them a wonderful hint of what it would mean to remain faithful to the One who was leading them. But as soon as they left Elim and faced the hard days in the wilderness again, they began to grumble once more. Water shortage wasn't their concern this time; now they wanted to know about food. Suddenly, the cruel hardships of Egypt were remembered as casual days of feasting and satisfaction. (This was less than two months after leaving behind their crushing role as slaves.) While we are shaking our heads over their fickle faith, we should pause to consider how quickly we forget the good things God does faithfully for us when we are faced with the things we don't like. Instead of seeing the "Marahs" of life as necessary challenges on the way to the "Elims," we expect God to fill our lives daily with "Elims" and keep us away

> ❝*We, like the Israelites, need to learn that it's not so much what we may be going through at any moment that counts as much as our awareness of who is going through it with us!*❞

from all "Marahs." But God persists in teaching us that on this side of the ultimate "Elim," when we are finally in His presence, we will all face His chosen mix of this life's "Marahs" and "Elims." We, like the Israelites, need to learn that it's not so much what we may be going through at any moment that counts as much as our awareness of who is going through it with us!

Instead of expressing confidence in God's ability and willingness to supply all their needs, the "default" outlook of Israel expressed deep-seated mistrust about God's intentions and Moses' role. Their motto was: When in doubt, doubt! So, when they noticed their traveling pantry getting empty, they grumbled. Instead of asking or even waiting, they complained. And God graciously provided manna by morning and quails by evening. He even gave them a double portion on the sixth day so they wouldn't have to work at gathering on the Sabbath. The daily regularity was broken up once a week to remind the people of their Provider. But even this simple lesson was tested (16:20, 27). Then, as soon as the people moved on in the Wilderness and reached dry Rephidim, they demanded water from Moses. Their attitude displayed no trace of grateful expectation. They were filled with "quarreling" and accusations against Moses' intentions. This lesson's key verse captures their outlook: "Is the Lᴏʀᴅ among us or not?" (17:7). Clearly they believed the answer to their bitter question was *not*. Yet God provided them with water from a rock, and Moses gave the place the dual name of Massah (testing) and Meribah (contention) as a reminder of the people's bad attitude.

About this time, the people whose territory Israel needed to cross on the way to the Promised Land (the Amalekites) decided to attack. These warlike, nomadic descendants of Esau would trouble the Israelites for centuries, but God declared through Moses that they sealed their fate by their unprovoked attack on God's people. And God taught Israel yet another lesson about His empowering presence even in the heat of battle. God used the wilderness passage in Israel's lives the same way He uses other kinds of wilderness experiences in our lives—to teach us about ourselves and train us to trust Him.

Express It

Pray today about the lessons in endurance that God has scattered throughout your life. How have you benefited from learning to trust Him? "When in doubt, doubt" sounds like an accurate description of our typical responses to life's challenges. What motto would better express your desire to remain steadfast in trusting God?

Consider It

As you read Exodus 15:1–17:16, consider these questions:

1) How does the song of Israel (chapter 15) describe God?

2) What threatening "horses" and "riders" have you experienced in your life?

3) How has God helped you deal with those problems or challenges?

4) In chapters 15 through 17 God meets the needs of Israel in several different ways. What are they, and what do you think God would have done if the people hadn't complained?

5) How did Moses handle these leadership challenges?

6) What insights do you draw from Moses' need for assistance during the battle with Amalek?

7) How has God used "wilderness" passages in your life?

Lesson

8

Meeting God

Moses, the great leader of Israel, had a couple of significant accountability relationships. First, he had God, who called him to this task. Second, he had his father-in-law, Jethro, a wise leader in his own right. In these two chapters, Moses had crucial interactions with both his mentors.

Read Exodus 18:1–19:25

Jethro's Advice

18 Jethro, the priest of Midian, Moses' father-in-law, heard of all that God had done for Moses and for Israel his people, how the Lord had brought Israel out of Egypt. ²Now Jethro, Moses' father-in-law, had taken Zipporah, Moses' wife, after he had sent her home, ³along with her two sons. The name of the one was Gershom (for he said, "I have been a sojourner in a foreign land"), ⁴and the name of the other, Eliezer (for he said, "The God of my father was my help, and delivered me from the sword of Pharaoh"). ⁵Jethro, Moses' father-in-law, came with his sons and his wife to Moses in the wilderness where he was encamped at the mountain of God. ⁶And when he sent word to Moses, "I, your father-in-law Jethro, am coming to you with your wife and her two sons with her," ⁷Moses went out to meet his father-in-law and bowed down and kissed him. And they asked each other of their welfare and went into the tent. ⁸Then Moses told his father-in-law all that the Lord had done to Pharaoh and to the Egyptians for Israel's sake, all the hardship that had come upon them in the way, and how the Lord had delivered them. ⁹And Jethro rejoiced for all the good that the Lord had done to Israel, in that he had delivered them out of the hand of the Egyptians.

¹⁰Jethro said, "Blessed be the Lord, who has delivered you out of the hand of the Egyptians and out of the hand of Pharaoh and has delivered the people from under the hand of the Egyptians. ¹¹Now I know that the Lord is greater than all gods, because in this affair they dealt arrogantly with the people." ¹²And Jethro, Moses' father-in-law, brought a burnt offering and sacrifices to God; and Aaron came with all the elders of Israel to eat bread with Moses' father-in-law before God.

> # Key Verse
>
> And the Lord said to Moses, "Behold, I am coming to you in a thick cloud, that the people may hear when I speak with you, and may also believe you forever" (Ex. 19:9).

¹³The next day Moses sat to judge the people, and the people stood around Moses from morning till evening. ¹⁴When Moses' father-in-law saw all that he was doing for the people, he said, "What is this that you are doing for the people? Why do you sit alone, and all the people stand around you from morning till evening?" ¹⁵And Moses said to his father-in-law, "Because the people come to me to inquire of God; ¹⁶when they have a dispute, they come to me and I decide between one person and another, and I make them know the statutes of God and his laws." ¹⁷Moses' father-in-law said to him, "What you are doing is not good. ¹⁸You and the people with you will certainly wear yourselves out, for the thing is too heavy for you. You are not able to do it alone. ¹⁹Now obey my voice; I will give you advice, and God be with you! You shall represent the people before God and bring their cases to God, ²⁰and you shall warn them about the statutes and the laws, and make them know the way in which they must walk and what they must do. ²¹Moreover, look for able men from all the people, men who fear God, who are trustworthy and hate a bribe, and place such men over the people as chiefs of thousands, of hundreds, of fifties, and of tens. ²²And

let them judge the people at all times. Every great matter they shall bring to you, but any small matter they shall decide themselves. So it will be easier for you, and they will bear the burden with you. ²³If you do this, God will direct you, you will be able to endure, and all this people also will go to their place in peace."

²⁴So Moses listened to the voice of his father-in-law and did all that he had said. ²⁵Moses chose able men out of all Israel and made them heads over the people, chiefs of thousands, of hundreds, of fifties, and of tens. ²⁶And they judged the people at all times. Any hard case they brought to Moses, but any small matter they decided themselves. ²⁷Then Moses let his father-in-law depart, and he went away to his own country.

Israel at Mount Sinai

19 On the third new moon after the people of Israel had gone out of the land of Egypt, on that day they came into the wilderness of Sinai. ²They set out from Rephidim and came into the wilderness of Sinai, and they encamped in the wilderness. There Israel encamped before the mountain, ³while Moses went up to God. The Lord called to him out of the mountain, saying, "Thus you shall say to the house of Jacob, and tell the people of Israel: ⁴You yourselves have seen what I did to the Egyptians, and how I bore you on eagles' wings and brought you to myself. ⁵Now therefore, if you will indeed obey my voice and keep my covenant, you shall be my treasured possession among all peoples, for all the earth is mine; ⁶and you shall be to me a kingdom of priests and a holy nation. These are the words that you shall speak to the people of Israel."

⁷So Moses came and called the elders of the people and set before them all these words that the Lord had commanded him. ⁸All the people answered together and said, "All that the Lord has spoken we will do." And

Moses reported the words of the people to the Lord. ⁹And the Lord said to Moses, "Behold, I am coming to you in a thick cloud, that the people may hear when I speak with you, and may also believe you forever."

When Moses told the words of the people to the Lord, ¹⁰the Lord said to Moses, "Go to the people and consecrate them today and tomorrow, and let them wash their garments ¹¹and be ready for the third day. For on the third day the Lord will come down on Mount Sinai in the sight of all the people. ¹²And you shall set limits for the people all around, saying, 'Take care not to go up into the mountain or touch the edge of it. Whoever touches the mountain shall be put to death. ¹³No hand shall touch him, but he shall be stoned or shot; whether beast or man, he shall not live.' When the trumpet sounds a long blast, they shall come up to the mountain." ¹⁴So Moses went down from the mountain to the people and consecrated the people; and they washed their garments. ¹⁵And he said to the people, "Be ready for the third day; do not go near a woman."

¹⁶On the morning of the third day there were thunders and lightnings and a thick cloud on the mountain and a very loud trumpet blast, so that all the people in the camp trembled. ¹⁷Then Moses brought the people out of the camp to meet God, and they took their stand at the foot of the mountain. ¹⁸Now Mount Sinai was wrapped in smoke because the Lord had descended on it in fire. The smoke of it went up like the smoke of a kiln, and the whole mountain trembled greatly. ¹⁹And as the sound of the trumpet grew louder and louder, Moses spoke, and God answered him in thunder. ²⁰The Lord came down on Mount Sinai, to the top of the mountain. And the Lord called Moses to the top of the mountain, and Moses went up.

²¹And the Lord said to Moses, "Go down and warn the people, lest they break through to the Lord to look and

many of them perish. ²²Also let the priests who come near to the LORD consecrate themselves, lest the LORD break out against them." ²³And Moses said to the LORD, "The people cannot come up to Mount Sinai, for you yourself warned us, saying, 'Set limits around the mountain and consecrate it.'" ²⁴And the LORD said to him, "Go down, and come up bringing Aaron with you. But do not let the priests and the people break through to come up to the LORD, lest he break out against them." ²⁵So Moses went down to the people and told them.

Go Deeper

The encounter between Israel and her God at Sinai was a solemn and awesome assembly. Formal protocol reveals the significance of the action. The stage was set when Israel arrived at the mountain and set up camp (Ex. 19:2–3). Moses approached the mountain, and God spoke, describing the agenda for the gathering (vv. 3–6). Then people responded, "All that the LORD has spoken we will do" (v. 8). The summit got underway when God came down with the effects described in Exodus 19:16–20. Everyone took their places for what was to follow: God's great declaration of His Commandments for His people.

In the New Testament, this great moment is recalled in Hebrews 12:18–29. The passage follows the great chapter on the heroes of the faith (Heb. 11) and the central message of Jesus as the "founder and perfecter of our faith" (Heb. 12:2). The writer of Hebrews built the case that Jesus changes everything and makes it even better. Like the ancient Israelites we, too, meet God but the atmosphere has been changed. Instead of a place of terror before a holy God, we come to "Mount Zion and to the city of the living God" (Heb. 12:22). And we come to Jesus. Things will be shaken again, but those in Christ have a "kingdom that cannot be shaken" (Heb. 12:28). We need to listen to Christ even more attentively than the Israelites did to God's voice at Sinai.

Even several thousand years ago, news traveled fast in the desert. The more fantastic the story, the more quickly it got around. Moses' father-in-law received word of the amazing events that had transpired in Egypt. One of the world's greatest powers had been crippled, humiliated, and defeated by the God of the Israelites. Jethro knew that those events had begun to unfold when his son-in-law, Moses, went back to Egypt under God's direction. Once he found out where the wandering nation was headed, Jethro decided to pay Moses a visit. Among other things, he could make sure Moses was reunited with his wife Zipporah (Jethro's daughter) and their two sons.

Moses welcomed Jethro with honor. Jethro responded with a public acknowledgment of Israel's God: "Now I know that the LORD is greater than all gods, because in this affair they dealt arrogantly with the people" (Ex. 18:11). Jethro the Midianite offered sacrifices to the Lord, and the Lord clearly accepted them. Jethro represents a stream of people we note throughout the Old Testament who knew God.

Jethro must have been impressed with his son-in-law's success, but he soon became concerned over his organizational style. Jethro could see that Moses had a problem with micro-management. He was trying personally to meet the needs of a nation. When he asked some pointed questions, Jethro uncovered Moses' failure to include delegation in his approach to leading Israel. Moses desperately needed the wisdom Jethro offered him: "Moses' father-in-law said to him, 'What you are doing is not good. You and the people with you will certainly wear yourselves out, for the thing is too heavy for you. You are not able to do it alone'" (18:17–18). Jethro helped Moses realize that his main task was to represent God to the nation and the nation to God, not to deal at the individual level with countless personal situations. Jethro's consultation set Moses free to pursue his primary purpose as God's leader for Israel.

Chapter 19 begins with Israel's approach to Mount Sinai, God's mountain. God chose this location to bring formally into being a nation: "Now therefore, if you will indeed obey my voice and keep my covenant, you shall be my treasured possession among all peoples, for all the earth is mine; and you shall be to me a kingdom of priests

"The fear of the Lord keeps us from ever becoming too casual or complacent in the way we speak about God and the way we address Him. This flows out of our experience of God's awe-inspiring greatness, holiness, justice, and power."

and a holy nation" (19:5–6). Thus began the great summit gathering between the recently freed slave nation and her God. Before God gave them His Law, He gave them His special presence, descending on Mount Sinai in a great cloud.

This event gives us a vivid example of what the Bible means when it talks about the fear of the Lord. The visual and sound effects that day had a definite effect: "All the people in the camp trembled" (19:16). God got their attention. And He wanted to make sure the awe didn't give way to curiosity. Everyone saw and heard; not everyone was allowed to approach. God retains the right to decide how close we can come. He wants us to "draw near" (James 4:8) and even "with confidence draw near to the throne of grace" (Heb. 4:16), but God never wants us to forget that we come by invitation and permission, not by right. The roles remain clear—God is God, and we are not. Moses was instructed to come into God's presence and to bring certain others, like Aaron (Ex. 19:24), with him, but the people were restrained at the bottom of the mountain. And even there God expected certain standards of conduct, "lest the LORD break out against them" (19:22).

The fear of the Lord keeps us from ever becoming too casual or complacent in the way we speak about God and the way we address Him. This flows out of our experience of God's awe-inspiring greatness, holiness, justice, and power. It results in our taking seriously certain of the Commandments, like treating God's name with respect. The fear of the Lord also prevents us from having any other gods or creating any other gods to replace Him.

God knew His people like He knows us. Few of them were ready to meet God. They may have trembled before God's awesome power, but they didn't fear Him in the right way. How else can we explain what happened among the people as Moses and God spoke on the mountain? God was right in keeping His people at a distance. They still had a lot to learn about walking with God. And many of them never learned!

Express It

As you pray, consider how you listen for God's voice. When you read God's Word, do you act as if He is speaking to you? Are you attentive and eager to obey? Ask God to keep you from the kind of quick agreement the Israelites were willing to make even though their hearts were actually far from God.

Consider It

As you read Exodus 18:1–19:25, consider these questions:

1) Describe Moses' relationship with his father-in-law. How did both of them benefit?

_____

_____

_____

2) What were the meanings behind the names Moses gave his sons?

_____

_____

_____

3) Why was Jethro's advice to Moses both timely and wise?

_____

_____

_____

4) How did God state His right to make a nation out of the Israelites?

_____

_____

_____

5) What did God tell the people to do to prepare for His special arrival? Why was this significant?

_____

_____

_____

6) In what different ways did God announce His presence on the mountain?

_____

_____

_____

7) How do the phrases "break through" (19:21) and "break out" (19:22) refer to two sides of the same situation between God and His people?

_____

_____

_____

The Ten Commandments

What is it about the Ten Commandments that causes such controversy? Legal battles over their posting in public places have occurred. Why do these words from God provoke such resistance from people?

Read Exodus 20:1–23:33

Exodus 20:1–26

The Ten Commandments

20 And God spoke all these words, saying,

²"I am the LORD your God, who brought you out of the land of Egypt, out of the house of slavery.

³"You shall have no other gods before me.

⁴"You shall not make for yourself a carved image, or any likeness of anything that is in heaven above, or that is in the earth beneath, or that is in the water under the earth. ⁵You shall not bow down to them or serve them, for I the LORD your God am a jealous God, visiting the iniquity of the fathers on the children to the third and the fourth generation of those who hate me, ⁶but showing steadfast love to thousands of those who love me and keep my commandments.

⁷"You shall not take the name of the LORD your God in vain, for the LORD will not hold him guiltless who takes his name in vain.

⁸"Remember the Sabbath day, to keep it holy. ⁹Six days you shall labor, and do all your work, ¹⁰but the seventh day is a Sabbath to the LORD your God. On it you shall not do any work, you, or your son, or your daughter, your male servant, or your female servant, or your livestock, or the sojourner who is within your gates. ¹¹For in six days the LORD made heaven and earth, the sea, and all that is in them, and rested on the seventh day. Therefore the LORD blessed the Sabbath day and made it holy.

¹²"Honor your father and your mother, that your days may be long in the land that the LORD your God is giving you.

¹³"You shall not murder.

¹⁴"You shall not commit adultery.

¹⁵"You shall not steal.

¹⁶"You shall not bear false witness against your neighbor.

> # Key Verse
>
> *Moses said to the people, "Do not fear, for God has come to test you, that the fear of him may be before you, that you may not sin"* (Ex. 20:20).

¹⁷"You shall not covet your neighbor's house; you shall not covet your neighbor's wife, or his male servant, or his female servant, or his ox, or his donkey, or anything that is your neighbor's."

¹⁸Now when all the people saw the thunder and the flashes of lightning and the sound of the trumpet and the mountain smoking, the people were afraid and trembled, and they stood far off ¹⁹and said to Moses, "You speak to us, and we will listen; but do not let God speak to us, lest we die." ²⁰Moses said to the people, "Do not fear, for God has come to test you, that the fear of him may be before you, that you may not sin." ²¹The people stood far off, while Moses drew near to the thick darkness where God was.

Laws About Altars

²²And the LORD said to Moses, "Thus you shall say to the people of Israel: 'You have seen for yourselves that I have talked with you from heaven. ²³You shall not make gods of silver to be with me, nor shall you make for yourselves gods of gold. ²⁴An altar of earth you shall make for me and sacrifice on it your burnt offerings and your peace offerings, your sheep and your oxen. In every place where I cause my name to be remembered I will come to you and bless

you. 25If you make me an altar of stone, you shall not build it of hewn stones, for if you wield your tool on it you profane it. 26And you shall not go up by steps to my altar, that your nakedness be not exposed on it.'"

Go Deeper

Two words are often used to describe our relationship with the Ten Commandments. We speak of *breaking* them or *keeping* them. What do these terms really mean? Can we *break* the Ten Commandments or do we find that we actually break ourselves on them? We read in Exodus 32:19 that Moses broke the original stone tables on which God had written the Ten Commandments, but even then, Moses didn't break the laws God had written. Can we *keep* the Commandments, or do we find that they actually keep us—keep us on track, keep us from sin, keep us from ruining our lives?

Usually, the context tells us that *keeping* means "doing," "obeying," "following" and "honoring." See, for example, such passages as Exodus 15:26; 16:28; 19:5; 20:6. Note how Jesus used the word *keep* in verses such as Luke 11:28; John 14:15, 23, 24; and 15:10. *Keeping* doesn't mean just knowing or having; it means "putting into practice for the right reasons."

Breaking conveys the idea of disobedience, a separation from and a treating of God's commandments as unimportant. When we speak of breaking God's commands, we are describing an action that takes a person from right living to wrong living. Breaking doesn't invalidate or change the commandments of God; it changes us. For an example of this process see Psalm 89:31–34. Take careful note of Jesus' words in Matthew 5:19 regarding God's commands.

When Jesus said that not even a punctuation mark from His Word would pass away (Matt. 5:18), He was pointing to the absolute nature of God's Word. It remains true and in force whether we keep it, ignore it, distort it, or forget it.

Engraved on granite monuments, embellished on parchment manuscripts, and embroidered into woven tapestries, the Ten Commandments have stood the test of time. Forget about the movie for a moment and imagine what it was like to be present when God delivered the summary of His purposes for humanity. Eventually the people saw God's laws written on stone tables. But first they heard and saw the evidence of God's presence.

God started with four laws related to Israel's dealings with Him. Law five highlights the relationship between parents and children. Laws six through ten guide our dealings with our neighbors. Nine of the laws are stated as negatives—only the child-parent relationship receives a direct positive. All ten read as clear and uncomplicated commands. God was not the least bit tentative when He declared His commandments. They are certain and absolute.

The absolute tone of the Ten Commandments provides a clue to why so many people instinctively resist them. That resistance has become more obvious in recent times with the rise of almost universal doubts about the possibility of absolutes. In a world where the difference between right and wrong has become more and more blurred, the Ten Commandments ring a jarring note of uncompromising truth that people don't want to hear or think about. Humans, including the Israelites who first received God words, have always cringed before the Ten Commandments. These decrees immediately point out flaws in us we don't want to face. Isn't it interesting that immediately following God's declaration, the people asked Moses to speak for God because they were afraid to listen to God directly, lest they die (Ex. 20:18–19). The first hearers made the same mistake that people are still making regarding the Ten Commandments. People still treat them as if ignoring them will somehow make them less devastatingly true. *Out of sight* might seem to help keep them *out of mind,* but it won't remove the fact that God has revealed His moral will, and we all fall short.

People who treat the Ten Commandments seriously fall into two groups. The first group believes that God gave us these commandments so that we would live up to them; the second group

> *"If our motivation for keeping the Ten Commandments is the pursuit of perfection, we will fail. But if our motivation for keeping the commandments is our fear and love for God, we'll actually do much better because we are not trying to earn God's acceptance by our performance. Instead, we are acknowledging God's love for us and responding to that love by living our lives to please Him."*

believes God gave us these commandments so that we would fear Him. The first group sees the commandments as a standard we can live up to, but the only way they can maintain that belief is to either soften the commandments or put them on a sliding scale that God uses to grade on the curve. The rich, young ruler whom Jesus met on the road was part of the first group (Matt. 19:16–22). When Jesus told him to keep the commandments, he responded, "Which ones?" Jesus listed several, to which the man said, "All these I have kept. What do I still lack?" (Matt. 19:20). Jesus didn't question his truthfulness; He simply helped the young man discover at least one of the ten he wasn't keeping—his wealth was more important to him than being right with God.

The second group who treat the Ten Commandments seriously believes God gave them to drive us to Him. Note what Moses told the people when they wanted to distance themselves from God: "Do not fear, for God has come to test you, that the fear of him may be before you, that you may not sin" (Ex. 20:20). The Ten Commandments are an absolute standard. They provide us with categories of obedience but also point out our inability to be perfect. If our motivation for keeping the Ten Commandments is the pursuit of perfection, we will fail. But if our motivation for keeping the commandments is our fear and love for God, we'll actually do much better because we are not trying to earn God's acceptance by our performance. Instead, we are acknowledging God's love for us and responding to that love by living our lives to please Him.

The first group (consciously or unconsciously) tries to earn God's acceptance and love by keeping the commandments. This is an impossible mission. The second group accepts God's love at the outset and then undertakes the task of letting the Holy Spirit live out the Ten Commandments through them as an expression of gratitude to God. Meanwhile, the world in general fears the absolute tone of the Ten Commandments because they don't know or understand the absolute love of the God who gave us those Commandments.

Express It

The classic hymn "Trust and Obey" captures the special relationship followers of Jesus have with all of God's commands. God calls us to trust Him and obey His commands. He wants us to obey because we know He is trustworthy rather than to obey out of terror or the belief that we are earning something from Him by obedience. As you meditate on the Ten Commandments, talk to the Lord about the levels of trust and obedience in your life right now.

Consider It

As you read Exodus 20:1–23:33, consider these questions:

1) Which of the Ten Commandments do you find the most personally challenging?

_____

_____

_____

2) What two kinds of fear is Moses talking about in Exodus 20:20?

_____

_____

_____

3) In what general ways do the specific laws of Exodus 20:22–23:33 relate to the Ten Commandments?

_____

_____

_____

4) What principles stand out for you in the rules about slaves and marriage (Ex. 21:1–11)?

_____

_____

_____

5) How do the laws about violence and accidents (Ex. 21:12–22:15) strike you as effective even today?

_____

_____

_____

6) Which of these many specific laws do you find most remarkable and why?

_____

_____

_____

7) How does the content of Exodus 23:32–33 take you back to the beginning of the Ten Commandments?

_____

_____

_____

The Covenant and the Tabernacle

God not only wanted to create a nation out of the people of Israel, He also wanted to create a holy and distinct group in the world through which He could present Himself to all peoples. After giving the Ten Commandments, God continued by describing how His people should worship.

Read Exodus 24:1–27:21

Exodus 24:1–25:22

The Covenant Confirmed

24 Then he said to Moses, "Come up to the Lord, you and Aaron, Nadab, and Abihu, and seventy of the elders of Israel, and worship from afar. ²Moses alone shall come near to the Lord, but the others shall not come near, and the people shall not come up with him."

³Moses came and told the people all the words of the Lord and all the rules. And all the people answered with one voice and said, "All the words that the Lord has spoken we will do." ⁴And Moses wrote down all the words of the Lord. He rose early in the morning and built an altar at the foot of the mountain, and twelve pillars, according to the twelve tribes of Israel. ⁵And he sent young men of the people of Israel, who offered burnt offerings and sacrificed peace offerings of oxen to the Lord. ⁶And Moses took half of the blood and put it in basins, and half of the blood he threw against the altar. ⁷Then he took the Book of the Covenant and read it in the hearing of the people. And they said, "All that the Lord has spoken we will do, and we will be obedient." ⁸And Moses took the blood and threw it on the people and said, "Behold the blood of the covenant that the Lord has made with you in accordance with all these words."

⁹Then Moses and Aaron, Nadab, and Abihu, and seventy of the elders of Israel went up, ¹⁰and they saw the God of Israel. There was under his feet as it were a pavement of sapphire stone, like the very heaven for clearness. ¹¹And he did not lay his hand on the chief men of the people of Israel; they beheld God, and ate and drank.

¹²The Lord said to Moses, "Come up to me on the mountain and wait there, that I may give you the tablets of stone, with the law and the commandment, which I have written for their instruction." ¹³So

---

> # Key Verse
>
> *And Moses took the blood and threw it on the people and said, "Behold the blood of the covenant that the Lord has made with you in accordance with all these words" (Ex.24:8).*

Moses rose with his assistant Joshua, and Moses went up into the mountain of God. ¹⁴And he said to the elders, "Wait here for us until we return to you. And behold, Aaron and Hur are with you. Whoever has a dispute, let him go to them."

¹⁵Then Moses went up on the mountain, and the cloud covered the mountain. ¹⁶The glory of the Lord dwelt on Mount Sinai, and the cloud covered it six days. And on the seventh day he called to Moses out of the midst of the cloud. ¹⁷Now the appearance of the glory of the Lord was like a devouring fire on the top of the mountain in the sight of the people of Israel. ¹⁸Moses entered the cloud and went up on the mountain. And Moses was on the mountain forty days and forty nights.

Contributions for the Sanctuary

25 The Lord said to Moses, ²"Speak to the people of Israel, that they take for me a contribution. From every man whose heart moves him you shall receive the contribution for me. ³And this is the contribution that you shall receive from them: gold, silver, and bronze, ⁴blue and purple and scarlet yarns and fine twined linen, goats' hair, ⁵tanned rams' skins, goatskins, acacia wood, ⁶oil for the lamps, spices for the anointing oil and for the fragrant incense, ⁷onyx stones, and stones for setting, for the ephod and for the breastpiece. ⁸And let them make me a sanctuary, that I may dwell in their midst. ⁹Exactly as I show you concerning the pattern of the tabernacle, and of all its furniture, so you shall make it.

The Ark of the Covenant

¹⁰"They shall make an ark of acacia wood. Two cubits and a half shall be its length, a cubit and a half its breadth, and a cubit and a half its height. ¹¹You shall overlay it with pure gold, inside and outside shall you overlay it, and you shall make on it a molding of gold around it. ¹²You shall cast four rings of gold for it and put them on its four feet, two rings on the one side of it, and two rings on the other side of it. ¹³You shall make poles of acacia wood and overlay them with gold. ¹⁴And you shall put the poles into the rings on the sides of the ark to carry the ark by them. ¹⁵The poles shall remain in the rings of the ark; they shall not be taken from it. ¹⁶And you shall put into the ark the testimony that I shall give you.

¹⁷"You shall make a mercy seat of pure gold. Two cubits and a half shall be its length, and a cubit and a half its breadth. ¹⁸And you shall make two cherubim of gold; of hammered work shall you make them, on the two ends of the mercy seat. ¹⁹Make one cherub on the one end, and one cherub on the other end. Of one piece with the mercy seat shall you make the cherubim on its two ends. ²⁰The cherubim shall spread out their wings above, overshadowing the mercy seat with their wings, their faces one to another; toward the mercy seat shall the faces of the cherubim be. ²¹And you shall put the mercy seat on the top of the ark, and in the ark you shall put the testimony that I shall give you. ²²There I will meet with you, and from above the mercy seat, from between the two cherubim that are on the ark of the testimony, I will speak with you about all that I will give you in commandment for the people of Israel."

Go Deeper

Take some time with a study Bible and a Bible dictionary to familiarize yourself with the various components of the original Sinai tabernacle. Even the engineering of the various parts is fascinating. Your understanding of this passage, the rest of Exodus, and much of Leviticus and Numbers will be deepened if you have a clear idea in your mind of this obvious structure in the middle of the Israelite camp that created a physical intersection between God and man.

Read Hebrews 8–9 for an introduction of the New Testament view of the tabernacle. The writer explains that God's insistence on exact obedience in constructing the tent and its furniture had a divine purpose. The tabernacle wasn't simply a temporary structure for use until a proper temple could be constructed; the tabernacle was a temporary structure that pointed to God's ultimate covenant with man in Christ. The ancient priests "serve a copy and shadow of the heavenly things. For when Moses was about to erect the tent, he was instructed by God, saying, 'See that you make everything according to the pattern that was shown you on the mountain'" (Heb. 8:5).

(continued)

Go Deeper Continued . . .

Even Solomon's great Temple and its replacement (the one constructed by Zerubbabel, which was later expanded and made more extravagant by Herod) only offered the illusion of permanence. All of them were destroyed. Jesus was pointing to the fact that the connection between God and man wasn't in a temple of stone and wood when He stood in the Jerusalem temple and announced, "Destroy this temple, and in three days I will raise it up" (John 2:19). See John 2:20–22 for His reasons.

T he word *covenant* is rarely used outside religious settings today. Occasionally *covenant* comes up in discussions of real estate rules, but the term itself has been largely left to theological conversations about the covenant of marriage or the covenants between God and man that are recorded in Scripture. Though the term is not commonly used, other terms mean almost the same thing. We now speak of treaties, agreements, and the exchange of solemn promises. Sometimes even the word *contract* is used to explain covenants, but a contract is a cold legal document, whereas a covenant gets its power from the character of those reaching an agreement and their willingness to be held to their words.

Exodus 24 describes the confirmation of God's fourth great covenant mentioned in Scripture. The first was God's covenant with Adam and all humans (Gen. 3:15). In it God declared the permanent enmity between Satan and mankind that would affect the promised seed, Jesus, who would crush the serpent's head. The second covenant God established with Noah after the flood (Gen. 9:8–17) in which God gave His word to never again destroy the world by a flood. Later, when God chose Abraham, he established and renewed His third covenant with the patriarch (Gen. 15:12–21 and 17:1–14).

Every covenant needs a sign to authenticate it, like Noah's rainbow or Abraham's rite of circumcision of every male child throughout all generations. No Jew could be a part of the covenant

"God showed amazing grace in confirming a covenant with people He knew would be unfaithful. But isn't that what God does in pouring out undeserved grace in our lives today?"

without the sign. So, all who were absorbed into the life of the people of Abraham also were expected to undergo the sign of the covenant. That was a demonstration that everybody who was brought into a Jewish home would be under the covenant of Israel. So, what was the sign of the covenant at Sinai?

Two great signs highlight the covenant at Sinai—the Exodus and the Book of the Covenant. God rescued Israel from slavery and then gave her His commandments. Moses "wrote down all the words of the Lord" (Ex. 24:4). As He did with Noah and Abraham, God accomplished a great act of liberation and then gave Israel lasting signs of their unique relationship.

This section of Exodus is somewhat difficult to read because it weaves together five strands: (1) what God was saying, (2) what Moses was doing (going up and down the mountain), (3) what Moses was writing, (4) what Moses was verbally reporting to the people and (5) how the people were responding at various times. It helps to remember that Exodus 19–32 has written as a sequence of events, but some of these events were happening at the same time. While God was giving Moses all the instructions about the tabernacle, the people were gearing up for pagan worship. Several times the people responded to God's unfolding covenant with the words, "All that the Lord has spoken we will do" (19:8; 24:7). God showed amazing grace in confirming a covenant with people He knew would be unfaithful. But isn't that what God does in pouring out undeserved grace in our lives today?

The covenant at Sinai was confirmed with blood. Exodus 24:3–8 describes the details of the sealing of the agreement between God and His people. Like the formal covenant between God and Abraham that began the racial lineage of the Messiah, God used the sacrifice of animal life to highlight the importance of the agreement. Parts of the animals were incinerated and half the blood was used on the altar and half was sprinkled on the people. The blood on the altar represented God's willingness to accept a substitute life as a covering for the sins of the people; the blood sprinkled on the people represented their acknowledgment of sins. The entire ceremony created a memorable confirmation. As Moses said, "Behold the blood of the covenant that the LORD has made with you in accordance with all these words" (v. 8).

Chapters 25–27 describe the funding and the plans for the tabernacle, a tent-sanctuary erected among a traveling people. God's presence in the cloud and pillar of fire would rest on the tabernacle when Israel was camped. God allowed the people to honor Him with their offerings of the materials needed for constructing the tabernacle and its furnishings. God gave specific instructions for the design of the Ark of the Covenant, the table for bread, the golden lampstand, the tabernacle itself, and the bronze altar. All these instruments of worship had a special role to play in God's message to His people. God had already demonstrated He was with His people; now God created a special place where His people could meet with Him.

Express It

As you pray today, think about the "furniture" in your life. What are the experiences, trials, and components of your life over which you have no control? These appear to have been decided, allowed or planned by God as part of your personal development. Think about your attitude toward God's ultimate decisions over your life. What would you like to say to Him about your level of cooperation with what He is working out in you?

Consider It

As you read Exodus 24:1–27:21, consider these questions:

1) How was the blood that sealed the covenant supplied (Ex. 24:3–8)?

_____

_____

2) To what does "the Book of the Covenant" (Ex. 24:7) refer?

_____

_____

3) Whom did Moses leave in charge while he was with God on the mountain?

_____

_____

4) What items were on the list of contributions for the tabernacle (Ex. 25:3–7)?

_____

_____

5) What did God emphasize to Moses in verses like Exodus 25:9, 40? What does this indicate to you about God?

_____

_____

6) To what extent does God indicate the purpose or significance of each of the items described in this passage—the Ark, the table for bread, the golden lampstand, the tabernacle, and the bronze altar?

_____

_____

7) How do these items and instructions for worship differ from the ones with which you are most familiar?

_____

_____

8) In what ways does Jesus represent the items God described to Moses?

_____

_____

Divine Designs

Not only did God design the furniture and details for His tabernacle, He also designed the very clothes to be worn by the priests who served Him. God cares about details because He teaches lessons through them.

Read Exodus 28:1–31:18

Exodus 28:1–29:21

The Priests' Garments

28 "Then bring near to you Aaron your brother, and his sons with him, from among the people of Israel, to serve me as priests—Aaron and Aaron's sons, Nadab and Abihu, Eleazar and Ithamar. ²And you shall make holy garments for Aaron your brother, for glory and for beauty. ³You shall speak to all the skillful, whom I have filled with a spirit of skill, that they make Aaron's garments to consecrate him for my priesthood. ⁴These are the garments that they shall make: a breastpiece, an ephod, a robe, a coat of checker work, a turban, and a sash. They shall make holy garments for Aaron your brother and his sons to serve me as priests. ⁵They shall receive gold, blue and purple and scarlet yarns, and fine twined linen.

⁶"And they shall make the ephod of gold, of blue and purple and scarlet yarns, and of fine twined linen, skillfully worked. ⁷It shall have two shoulder pieces attached to its two edges, so that it may be joined together. ⁸And the skillfully woven band on it shall be made like it and be of one piece with it, of gold, blue and purple and scarlet yarns, and fine twined linen. ⁹You shall take two onyx stones, and engrave on them the names of the sons of Israel, six of their names on the one stone, and the names of the remaining six on the other stone, in the order of their birth. ¹¹As a jeweler engraves signets, so shall you engrave the two stones with the names of the sons of Israel. You shall enclose them in settings of gold filigree. ¹²And you shall set the two stones on the shoulder pieces of the ephod, as stones of remembrance for the sons of Israel. And Aaron shall bear their names before the Lord on his two shoulders for remembrance. ¹³You shall make settings of gold filigree, ¹⁴and two chains of pure gold, twisted like cords; and you shall attach the corded chains to the settings.

> # Key Verse
>
> *"And you shall gird Aaron and his sons with sashes and bind caps on them. And the priesthood shall be theirs by a statute forever. Thus you shall ordain Aaron and his sons"* (Ex. 29:9).

¹⁵"You shall make a breastpiece of judgment, in skilled work. In the style of the ephod you shall make it—of gold, blue and purple and scarlet yarns, and fine twined linen shall you make it. ¹⁶It shall be square and doubled, a span its length and a span its breadth. ¹⁷You shall set in it four rows of stones. A row of sardius, topaz, and carbuncle shall be the first row; ¹⁸and the second row an emerald, a sapphire, and a diamond; ¹⁹and the third row a jacinth, an agate, and an amethyst; ²⁰and the fourth row a beryl, an onyx, and a jasper. They shall be set in gold filigree. ²¹There shall be twelve stones with their names according to the names of the sons of Israel. They shall be like signets, each engraved with its name, for the twelve tribes. ²²You shall make for the breastpiece twisted chains like cords, of pure gold. ²³And you shall make for the breastpiece two rings of gold, and put the two rings on the two edges of the breastpiece. ²⁴And you shall put the two cords of gold in the two rings at the edges of the breastpiece. ²⁵The two ends of the two cords you shall attach to the two settings of filigree, and so attach it in front to the shoulder pieces of the ephod. ²⁶You shall make two rings of gold, and put them at the two ends of the breastpiece, on its inside edge next to the ephod. ²⁷And you shall make two

rings of gold, and attach them in front to the lower part of the two shoulder pieces of the ephod, at its seam above the skillfully woven band of the ephod. ²⁸And they shall bind the breastpiece by its rings to the rings of the ephod with a lace of blue, so that it may lie on the skillfully woven band of the ephod, so that the breastpiece shall not come loose from the ephod. ²⁹So Aaron shall bear the names of the sons of Israel in the breastpiece of judgment on his heart, when he goes into the Holy Place, to bring them to regular remembrance before the Lord. ³⁰And in the breastpiece of judgment you shall put the Urim and the Thummim, and they shall be on Aaron's heart, when he goes in before the Lord. Thus Aaron shall bear the judgment of the people of Israel on his heart before the Lord regularly.

³¹"You shall make the robe of the ephod all of blue. ³²It shall have an opening for the head in the middle of it, with a woven binding around the opening, like the opening in a garment, so that it may not tear. ³³On its hem you shall make pomegranates of blue and purple and scarlet yarns, around its hem, with bells of gold between them, ³⁴a golden bell and a pomegranate, a golden bell and a pomegranate, around the hem of the robe. ³⁵And it shall be on Aaron when he ministers, and its sound shall be heard when he goes into the Holy Place before the Lord, and when he comes out, so that he does not die.

³⁶"You shall make a plate of pure gold and engrave on it, like the engraving of a signet, 'Holy to the Lord.' ³⁷And you shall fasten it on the turban by a cord of blue. It shall be on the front of the turban. ³⁸It shall be on Aaron's forehead, and Aaron shall bear any guilt from the holy things that the people of Israel consecrate as their holy gifts. It shall regularly be on his forehead, that they may be accepted before the Lord.

³⁹"You shall weave the coat in checker work of fine linen, and you shall make a turban of fine linen, and you shall make a sash embroidered with needlework.

⁴⁰"For Aaron's sons you shall make coats and sashes and caps. You shall make them for glory and beauty. ⁴¹And you shall put them on Aaron your brother, and on his sons with him, and shall anoint them and ordain them and consecrate them, that they may serve me as priests. ⁴²You shall make for them linen undergarments to cover their naked flesh. They shall reach from the hips to the thighs; ⁴³and they shall be on Aaron and on his sons when they go into the tent of meeting or when they come near the altar to minister in the Holy Place, lest they bear guilt and die. This shall be a statute forever for him and for his offspring after him.

Consecration of the Priests

29 "Now this is what you shall do to them to consecrate them, that they may serve me as priests. Take one bull of the herd and two rams without blemish, ²and unleavened bread, unleavened cakes mixed with oil, and unleavened wafers smeared with oil. You shall make them of fine wheat flour. ³You shall put them in one basket and bring them in the basket, and bring the bull and the two rams. ⁴You shall bring Aaron and his sons to the entrance of the tent of meeting and wash them with water. ⁵Then you shall take the garments, and put on Aaron the coat and the robe of the ephod, and the ephod, and the breastpiece, and gird him with the skillfully woven band of the ephod. ⁶And you shall set the turban on his head and put the holy crown on the turban. ⁷You shall take the anointing oil and pour it on his head and anoint him. ⁸Then you shall bring his sons and put coats on them, ⁹and you shall gird Aaron and his sons with sashes and bind caps on them. And the priesthood shall be theirs by a statute forever. Thus you shall ordain Aaron and his sons.

¹⁰"Then you shall bring the bull before the tent of meeting. Aaron and his sons

shall lay their hands on the head of the bull. ¹¹Then you shall kill the bull before the Lord at the entrance of the tent of meeting, ¹²and shall take part of the blood of the bull and put it on the horns of the altar with your finger, and the rest of the blood you shall pour out at the base of the altar. ¹³And you shall take all the fat that covers the entrails, and the long lobe of the liver, and the two kidneys with the fat that is on them, and burn them on the altar. ¹⁴But the flesh of the bull and its skin and its dung you shall burn with fire outside the camp; it is a sin offering.

¹⁵"Then you shall take one of the rams, and Aaron and his sons shall lay their hands on the head of the ram, ¹⁶and you shall kill the ram and shall take its blood and throw it against the sides of the altar. ¹⁷Then you shall cut the ram into pieces, and wash its entrails and its legs, and put them with its pieces and its head, ¹⁸and burn the whole ram on the altar. It is a burnt offering to the Lord. It is a pleasing aroma, a food offering to the Lord.

¹⁹"You shall take the other ram, and Aaron and his sons shall lay their hands on the head of the ram, ²⁰and you shall kill the ram and take part of its blood and put it on the tip of the right ear of Aaron and on the tips of the right ears of his sons, and on the thumbs of their right hands and on the great toes of their right feet, and throw the rest of the blood against the sides of the altar. ²¹Then you shall take part of the blood that is on the altar, and of the anointing oil, and sprinkle it on Aaron and his garments, and on his sons and his sons' garments with him. He and his garments shall be holy, and his sons and his sons' garments with him.

Go Deeper

In Exodus 28:41, God instructed Moses to anoint, ordain, and consecrate Aaron and his sons. These three terms are used repeatedly throughout the passages related to Aaron and his sons' installation as the first in a line of priests who would serve in a special capacity for the people of Israel. The terms have some overlap in meaning, but they also point to specific parts of the process. "Anointing" had to do with the act of pouring or sprinkling something on a subject. In this case some of the anointing was done with an oil mixture and some with a blood mixture. "Ordaining" had to do with identifying for the people the special role to be carried out by the priest on their behalf. They were now men under orders from God, orders which they needed to carry out faithfully. "Consecration" had to do with delivering the anointed and ordained priests into God's hands. It set someone apart to God for service.

Notice how these terms are used in Exodus 29:1, 7–9, 21–22, 26, 29, 31; 30:25–30. As you read these passages, think about the ways in which we honor God's holiness today. What steps can you take in your personal life to treat God's character with proper respect and worship?

Somewhere among the tents and lean-tos of the camp of Israel, a craftsman named Bezalel had his workshop. He probably honed his skills under the demanding expectations of the Egyptian overseers. Pharaohs needed more than menial laborers making bricks and cutting stones for their monuments—they also needed able smiths in many skills to create the treasures that would one day amaze the world when the tombs of these Egyptian rulers were uncovered. Perhaps Bezalel had already been noticed for his special skills.

During His summit with Moses, God appointed Bezalel as the artist to carry out the detailed instructions God had given for the tabernacle, furnishings, and the clothing of the priests. We aren't told whether Moses knew Bezalel or his work, but this craftsman was about to become famous for his multi-faceted skills as an artist. God told Moses, "See, I have called by name Bezalel the son of Uri, son of Hur, of the tribe of Judah, and I have filled him with the Spirit of God, with ability and intelligence, with knowledge and all craftsmanship" (Ex. 31:2-3). God designed a particular man and then gave him a special job to do. God also provided Bezalel with an assistant, Oholiab (v. 6). It's worth noting that Bezalel came from the tribe of Judah, while Oholiab was a descendant of Dan. We will find out more about them in a future lesson.

According to Exodus 25-27 God specified some of the main furnishings and the structure of the tabernacle itself. As a result of the generosity of the people of Israel, the finest materials were provided for this special place and all its parts. Back in chapter 25:3-9, God listed the items that would be used for these purposes. It was clear that God's sanctuary would be a priceless object of great beauty, standing as a holy place among the people of Israel.

Beginning with Exodus 28, God described in great detail even the garments to be worn by those who served in and around the tabernacle. He set aside the tribe of Levi (Moses' family was from that tribe) to be perpetual servants of His on behalf of the people. The first of these would be Aaron, Moses' brother, and his four sons. The chosen priests would serve in a place of beauty, wearing costly garments that would highlight God's glory and worth. On his

"God wanted His people to be aware always of His presence. He had provided them with an abundance of resources and skills that they would be able to use in honoring Him. And once each week, on the Sabbath, the entire nation would focus on the God who had freed them and was guiding them to His Promised Land."

forehead Aaron wore a plate of pure gold on which was engraved the phrase "Holy to the LORD" (28:36). He carried as part of the priestly attire two special stones engraved with the names of the 12 tribes of Israel. These were mounted on a plate that covered his heart, symbolizing his call to pray for the people of Israel. He also carried the Urim and Thummim (v. 30), apparently precious stones the purpose of which was to help the priest determine God's will in matters. We are not certain how these worked, but they were part of the priest's responsibility.

Since the priest functioned as a mediator between God and man, he must not forget that he was charged with a holy office. He had to "dress the part," and he also had to be set aside through an elaborate and public anointment/ordination/consecration ceremony (see Go Deeper). The process of consecration involved at least four specific steps. First, the candidate was washed (29:4). Second, he was anointed with oil (29:7). Sacrifices were then made on his behalf (vv. 10–20), including a bull and two rams. Finally, part of the second ram's blood was mixed with anointing oil and sprinkled on the priest and his special clothing (vv. 19–20).

All of these details and the tone of warning in which they were given serve to highlight the holiness of God. Repeatedly, Aaron and his descendants were warned that carelessness with God's instructions would lead to death (28:35, 43). God's character required that those standing between Him and His people be continuously and cautiously aware of their privilege. They bore a solemn responsibility, and failure to take that responsibility seriously came with serious consequences.

Almost immediately Aaron and his sons were to begin a daily rhythm of sacrifices on behalf of the people. Exodus 29:38–46 describes the sunrise and sundown sacrifice of a lamb, grain, and drink as ongoing sacrifices to God who would "dwell among the people of Israel and will be their God" (29:45). God wanted His people to be aware always of His presence, whether it was through the continual aroma of incense, the daily sacrifices, or the census tax. He had provided them with an abundance of resources and skills that they would be able to use in honoring Him. And once each week, on the Sabbath, the entire nation would focus on the God who had freed them and was guiding them to His Promised Land.

Express It

As you pray, think about the objects in your life that point toward God's holiness. Your Bible, your church building, and the spiritual leaders in your life are all reminders of God's presence. Talk to God about the ways He lets you know He cares and is involved with you. Tell Him what you think of His holiness.

Consider It

As you read Exodus 28:1–31:18, consider these questions:

1) Why was God's holiness both awesome and threatening to man?

2) What is your visual impression of the priest dressed in God's designer vestments?

3) What ideas were emphasized in publicly consecrating the priests for service?

4) In what ways does the church preserve some of this solemn recognition of the role of spiritual leadership?

5) How does the church function differently today? Why is this?

6) Why do you think everyone's census tax (30:11–16) was the same amount, no matter what their status?

7) How does God's holiness affect the way you worship and live?

A Shameful Episode

Most people who know something about the Book of Exodus can name at least three significant events that occur in it: the crossing of the Red Sea, the giving of the Ten Commandments, and Israel's shocking worship of a golden calf. What can we learn from this temptation to idolatry?

Read Exodus 32:1—34:35
Exodus 32:1–35

The Golden Calf

32 When the people saw that Moses delayed to come down from the mountain, the people gathered themselves together to Aaron and said to him, "Up, make us gods who shall go before us. As for this Moses, the man who brought us up out of the land of Egypt, we do not know what has become of him." ²So Aaron said to them, "Take off the rings of gold that are in the ears of your wives, your sons, and your daughters, and bring them to me." ³So all the people took off the rings of gold that were in their ears and brought them to Aaron. ⁴And he received the gold from their hand and fashioned it with a graving tool and made a golden calf. And they said, "These are your gods, O Israel, who brought you up out of the land of Egypt!" ⁵When Aaron saw this, he built an altar before it. And Aaron made proclamation and said, "Tomorrow shall be a feast to the LORD." ⁶And they rose up early the next day and offered burnt offerings and brought peace offerings. And the people sat down to eat and drink and rose up to play.

⁷And the LORD said to Moses, "Go down, for your people, whom you brought up out of the land of Egypt, have corrupted themselves. ⁸They have turned aside quickly out of the way that I commanded them. They have made for themselves a golden calf and have worshiped it and sacrificed to it and said, 'These are your gods, O Israel, who brought you up out of the land of Egypt!'" ⁹And the LORD said to Moses, "I have seen this people, and behold, it is a stiff-necked people. ¹⁰Now therefore let me alone, that my wrath may burn hot against them and I may consume them, in order that I may make a great nation of you."

¹¹But Moses implored the LORD his God and said, "O LORD, why does your

---

> # Key Verse
>
> *And the LORD said to Moses, "Go down, for your people, whom you brought up out of the land of Egypt, have corrupted themselves"* (Ex. 32:7).

---

wrath burn hot against your people, whom you have brought out of the land of Egypt with great power and with a mighty hand? ¹²Why should the Egyptians say, 'With evil intent did he bring them out, to kill them in the mountains and to consume them from the face of the earth'? Turn from your burning anger and relent from this disaster against your people. ¹³Remember Abraham, Isaac, and Israel, your servants, to whom you swore by your own self, and said to them, 'I will multiply your offspring as the stars of heaven, and all this land that I have promised I will give to your offspring, and they shall inherit it forever.'" ¹⁴And the LORD relented from the disaster that he had spoken of bringing on his people.

¹⁵Then Moses turned and went down from the mountain with the two tablets of the testimony in his hand, tablets that were written on both sides; on the front and on the back they were written. ¹⁶The tablets were the work of God, and the writing was the writing of God, engraved on the tablets. ¹⁷When Joshua heard the noise of the people as they shouted, he said to Moses, "There is a noise of war in the camp." ¹⁸But he said, "It is not the sound of shouting for victory, or the sound of the cry of defeat, but the sound of singing that I hear." ¹⁹And as soon as he came near the camp and saw the calf and the dancing, Moses' anger burned hot, and he threw the tablets out of his

hands and broke them at the foot of the mountain. ²⁰He took the calf that they had made and burned it with fire and ground it to powder and scattered it on the water and made the people of Israel drink it.

²¹And Moses said to Aaron, "What did this people do to you that you have brought such a great sin upon them?" ²²And Aaron said, "Let not the anger of my lord burn hot. You know the people, that they are set on evil. ²³For they said to me, 'Make us gods who shall go before us. As for this Moses, the man who brought us up out of the land of Egypt, we do not know what has become of him.' ²⁴So I said to them, 'Let any who have gold take it off.' So they gave it to me, and I threw it into the fire, and out came this calf."

²⁵And when Moses saw that the people had broken loose (for Aaron had let them break loose, to the derision of their enemies), ²⁶then Moses stood in the gate of the camp and said, "Who is on the LORD's side? Come to me." And all the sons of Levi gathered around him. ²⁷And he said to them, "Thus says the LORD God of Israel, 'Put your sword on your side each of you, and go to and fro from gate to gate throughout the camp, and each

of you kill his brother and his companion and his neighbor.'" ²⁸And the sons of Levi did according to the word of Moses. And that day about three thousand men of the people fell. ²⁹And Moses said, "Today you have been ordained for the service of the LORD, each one at the cost of his son and of his brother, so that he might bestow a blessing upon you this day."

³⁰The next day Moses said to the people, "You have sinned a great sin. And now I will go up to the LORD; perhaps I can make atonement for your sin." ³¹So Moses returned to the LORD and said, "Alas, this people has sinned a great sin. They have made for themselves gods of gold. ³²But now, if you will forgive their sin—but if not, please blot me out of your book that you have written." ³³But the LORD said to Moses, "Whoever has sinned against me, I will blot out of my book. ³⁴But now go, lead the people to the place about which I have spoken to you; behold, my angel shall go before you. Nevertheless, in the day when I visit, I will visit their sin upon them."

³⁵Then the LORD sent a plague on the people, because they made the calf, the one that Aaron made.

Go Deeper

The stress of leadership wasn't easy for Moses, but it forged an amazing relationship between God and him. One of the most intimate verses in the Bible is found in this section: "Thus the LORD used to speak to Moses face to face, as a man speaks to his friend" (Ex. 33:11). Consider the parallels between Moses' spending time alone with God (33:7–11) and Jesus spending regular time alone with His Father (Mark 1:35–39).

Four times in these chapters Moses pleaded for God to remain present and forgive His people (Ex. 32:11–13, 31–32; 33:12–16; 34:8–9; see also Ps. 106:19–23). We don't know and are not told what would have happened if Moses hadn't pleaded for the people. But the Bible says, "The LORD relented from the disaster that he had spoken of bringing on his people" (Ex. 32:14). Some translations say, "The LORD repented,"

(continued)

Go Deeper Continued . . .

which doesn't mean that God had been planning something sinful. It just means He changed His mind in how He would handle His wayward people. His purpose remained unchanged. This is an example of God's willingness to be seen like us. The technical term for this is anthropopathism—God's ability to connect with human experiences such as sadness, anger, and tenderness. God doesn't change, but our understanding of His purposes and actions sometimes makes it seem that way.

The deep lesson in this passage is about the crucial nature of intercessory prayer. When we plead with God for others, we enter into God's work in their lives. One of the most effective ways we participate in bringing about God's will is through our own willingness to pray intently for others—even when they don't deserve it or realize it.

Moses had gone up the mountain. However, he was on the mountain so long that people believed he was never coming back. But the previous chapters, taken as an account of many things that happened simultaneously, indicate that Moses hadn't been gone all that long. In fact he had only been gone 40 days. These people had been in Egyptian bondage 430 years! Moses was out of sight 40 days, and they basically said to Aaron, "We don't know what's happened to him. He's probably never coming back. Make us a replacement—something in gold will do fine."

We don't know if Aaron was buying time or if he was just intimidated, but he took up a collection of gold jewelry and proceeded to fashion a golden calf. No sooner was he done than the people declared, "These are your gods, O Israel, who brought you up out of the land of Egypt!" (Ex. 32:4). This golden calf couldn't have been very large. But it was large enough that all the people could see it. And immediately they declared their new creation was a god. Just hours before this "god" had been their earrings.

Now, how foolish is that? Well, it's about as foolish as saying that you are your own god—or that you can create your own god to suit your needs. But isn't that exactly what many people are doing today? They casually claim they can create a workable religion on their own.

But Aaron added foolhardiness to foolishness when he said,

"Could it be that God sometimes puts difficult people in our pathway just to see what we are made of? Or could it be that God puts difficult people and situations in our pathway so we can discover what we're made of?"

"Tomorrow shall be a feast to the LORD" (32:5). Note that the word *LORD* is in all capital letters, something that indicates the personal name for the God of Israel, Yahweh. Aaron was trying to mix false religion with true religion. That's called syncretism, and God hates it. The results were catastrophic. The calf was out of the bag. The idol had instantly become an object of worship. While God was telling Moses on the mountain, "You shall not make for yourself a carved image" (Ex. 20:4–5), His people were busy doing exactly that down on the plain—along with obscene and immoral forms of worship (see Exodus 32:6, where "play" can mean "lewd entertainment" and has a sexual connotation).

Imagine Moses' shock when God suddenly said to him, "Go down, for your people, whom you brought up out of the land of Egypt, have corrupted themselves" (32:7). Moses was speechless! God made it clear that He didn't want to have anything to do with these people. He didn't say, "My people"; He said, "Your people." The people had corrupted themselves by creatively inventing new religious experiences (which were really the same old pagan rituals) to improve upon what God offered them. Religious experience is not something we put together like a recipe. Religious experience is when we discover who God is, and we relate to Him. That God doesn't change. If we know this truth and turn away from it, we corrupt ourselves as badly as the Israelites!

God went on to call them a quick-turning (32:8) and stiff-necked people (v. 9)! Then God finished with words that must have sent a chill down Moses' spine, "Now therefore let me alone, that my wrath may burn hot against them and I may consume them, in order that I may make a great nation of you" (v. 10). God's wrath had reached the point of incineration. He seemed about ready to end the nation-building project in a giant ball of flame.

God told Moses, "Here's a solution. I'll just kill them all." The same God who had appeared to Moses, perhaps on this same mountainside, in a fiery bush to send Moses into Egypt was now suggesting that Israel might be beyond rescue. Was God simply frustrated with events and surprised by the people's deep-seated sinfulness? Or did God say this to Moses because He intended to get Moses' response? Could it be that God sometimes puts difficult people in our pathway just to see what we are made of? Or could it be that God puts difficult people and situations in our pathway so we can discover what we're made of?

Was God surprised when Moses' pleaded for the people (vv. 11–13)? Or was Moses surprised by his own commitment to the people God had called Him to lead? They were God's people, yes, but they were also his people—his God-given responsibility. And now he was undergoing the ultimate test of that responsibility. He had to plead with God for the people's very existence. Notice how Moses became more decisive during the difficult days that followed (see Go Deeper). God turned this terrible crisis into a training exercise for the man He had chosen to lead His people.

Express It

For whom are you pleading with God? Who are the people in your life who are in desperate straits? How are you praying for them? Review the way Moses pleaded for Israel and let his approach shape the way you pray intently for others (see Go Deeper). Pray and watch God work.

Consider It

As you read Exodus 32:1–34:35, consider these questions:

1) What do Aaron's actions tell you about the continual reality of sinful temptation?

_____

_____

2) Why did the people turn to idolatry so quickly without Moses?

_____

_____

3) How long are we willing to "wait on the Lord" before we start trying to take matters into our own hands?

_____

_____

4) What were the deadly and painful consequences of this idolatrous event? See 32:25–29, 35.

_____

_____

5) How does the description of Moses' relationship with God (33:7–11) increase your longing for intimacy with God?

_____

_____

6) What do you think Moses discovered about himself during this terrible episode?

_____

_____

7) God wrote the Ten Commandments on stone tablets twice. How do the two circumstances compare?

_____

_____

8) What lessons about restoration can you identify in these chapters?

_____

_____

The Gift of Creativity

Creativity is expressed in two ways: by what a person does and by what a person helps others to do. God filled two men (Bezalel and Oholiab) with artistic and teaching skills that led to the creation of what was one of the wonders of the world.

Read Exodus 35:1–37:29
Exodus 35:1–35

Sabbath Regulations

35 Moses assembled all the congregation of the people of Israel and said to them, "These are the things that the LORD has commanded you to do. ²Six days work shall be done, but on the seventh day you shall have a Sabbath of solemn rest, holy to the LORD. Whoever does any work on it shall be put to death. ³You shall kindle no fire in all your dwelling places on the Sabbath day."

Contributions for the Tabernacle

⁴Moses said to all the congregation of the people of Israel, "This is the thing that the LORD has commanded. ⁵Take from among you a contribution to the LORD. Whoever is of a generous heart, let him bring the LORD's contribution: gold, silver, and bronze; ⁶blue and purple and scarlet yarns and fine twined linen; goats' hair, ⁷tanned rams' skins, and goatskins; acacia wood, ⁸oil for the light, spices for the anointing oil and for the fragrant incense, ⁹and onyx stones and stones for setting, for the ephod and for the breastpiece.

¹⁰"Let every skillful craftsman among you come and make all that the LORD has commanded: ¹¹the tabernacle, its tent and its covering, its hooks and its frames, its bars, its pillars, and its bases; ¹²the ark with its poles, the mercy seat, and the veil of the screen; ¹³the table with its poles and all its utensils, and the bread of the Presence; ¹⁴the lampstand also for the light, with its utensils and its lamps, and the oil for the light; ¹⁵and the altar of incense, with its poles, and the anointing oil and the fragrant incense, and the screen for the door, at the door of the tabernacle; ¹⁶the altar of burnt offering, with its grating of bronze, its poles, and all its utensils, the basin and its stand; ¹⁷the hangings of the court, its pillars and its bases, and the screen for the gate of the court; ¹⁸the pegs of the tabernacle and the pegs of the court, and their cords; ¹⁹the finely worked garments for ministering in the Holy Place, the holy garments for Aaron the priest, and the garments of his sons, for their service as priests."

²⁰Then all the congregation of the people of Israel departed from the presence of Moses. ²¹And they came, everyone whose heart stirred him, and everyone whose spirit moved him, and brought the LORD's contribution to be used for the tent of meeting, and for all its service, and for the holy garments. ²²So they came, both men and women. All who were of a willing heart brought brooches and earrings and signet rings and armlets, all sorts of gold objects, every man dedicating an offering of gold to the LORD. ²³And every one who possessed blue or purple or scarlet yarns or fine linen or goats' hair or tanned rams' skins or goatskins brought them. ²⁴Everyone who could make a contribution of silver or bronze brought it as the LORD's contribution. And every one who possessed acacia wood of any use in the work brought it. ²⁵And every skillful woman spun with her hands, and they all brought what they had spun in blue and purple and scarlet yarns and fine twined linen. ²⁶All the women whose hearts stirred them to use their skill spun the goats' hair. ²⁷And the leaders brought onyx stones and stones to be set, for

the ephod and for the breastpiece, ²⁸and spices and oil for the light, and for the anointing oil, and for the fragrant incense. ²⁹All the men and women, the people of Israel, whose heart moved them to bring anything for the work that the Lord had commanded by Moses to be done brought it as a freewill offering to the Lord.

Construction of the Tabernacle

³⁰Then Moses said to the people of Israel, "See, the Lord has called by name Bezalel the son of Uri, son of Hur, of the tribe of Judah; ³¹and he has filled him with the Spirit of God, with skill, with intelligence, with knowledge, and with

all craftsmanship, ³²to devise artistic designs, to work in gold and silver and bronze, ³³in cutting stones for setting, and in carving wood, for work in every skilled craft. ³⁴And he has inspired him to teach, both him and Oholiab the son of Ahisamach of the tribe of Dan. ³⁵He has filled them with skill to do every sort of work done by an engraver or by a designer or by an embroiderer in blue and purple and scarlet yarns and fine twined linen, or by a weaver—by any sort of workman or skilled designer.

Go Deeper

Paul summarized beautifully what it means to be a Christian when he wrote to the Ephesians, "For by grace you have been saved through faith. And this is not your own doing; it is the gift of God, not a result of works, so that no one may boast. For we are his workmanship, created in Christ Jesus for good works, which God prepared beforehand, that we should walk in them" (Eph. 2:8–10). If we are followers of Jesus, the new life in us is evidence of the Holy Spirit's indwelling. The gift of salvation is provided by Christ and delivered to us by God's Spirit. We are no longer trying to produce something with our lives that will cause God to accept us; we now realize that we can live our lives in gratitude and productivity because of what Christ has done for us.

We don't do good works so God will love us; we engage in good works because God loves us!

For a Christian, creative exactness means discovering what God wants us to do with our lives and then asking Him to help us use what He has given us to create something beautiful for Him. We (our bodies) are more like a tabernacle than a temple (for instance, we move; see 1 Cor. 3:16–17 and 6:19.) Elsewhere, Paul confirms this when he says, "For we know that if the tent that is our earthly home is destroyed, we have a building from God, a house not made with hands, eternal in the heavens" (2 Cor. 5:1). While our "tent" is standing, let's be creatively exact in living as God wants us to live.

The most frequent phrase in these three chapters of Exodus is "he made." The "he" refers to the man named Bezalel, who would probably be ranked with other artists like Da Vinci and Michelangelo if any of his work was still in existence. His work was not only beautiful, but it was also utilitarian. He was the ultimate tentmaker. He built a structure as elaborate and lovely as the greatest cathedral and yet as movable as a nomad's home. Bezalel had a mind given over to God so as to bring about the structure and furniture God would call His own dwelling in the desert. The tabernacle whose construction Bezalel oversaw lasted for at least 500 years. The last time its location is mentioned is in Gibeon, where it was still standing after David brought the Ark of the Covenant to Jerusalem (1 Chron. 21:29). Among his final declarations, David said, "The LORD, the God of Israel, has given rest to his people, and he dwells in Jerusalem forever. And so the Levites no longer need to carry the tabernacle or any of the things for its service" (1 Chron. 23:25–26).

This lesson's key verse summarizes God's gift to Bezalel. He was filled with one Spirit and four by-products of that filling: skill, intelligence, knowledge, and craftsmanship. Skill has to do with performing the work and showing others how to do it. Intelligence has to do with grasping an idea and seeing what skills are needed to accomplish it. Knowledge has to do with an awareness of certain fields or media so that skill and intelligence accomplish their most effective work. And craftsmanship is that almost magic quality that allows certain people to create complex structures or works of art in any media that "succeed" in unexpected ways. In the case of the tabernacle and its furnishings, things had to succeed in the way they looked, succeed in the way they served specific purposes, and succeed in the way they could be transported from one campsite to the next. We're also told that Bezalel and Oholiab were "inspired to teach" (Ex. 35:34). God's Spirit allowed them to extend their gifts to others.

There are several aspects to Bezalel's work that are worth highlighting. First, it was commissioned work. Second, it was creatively exact work. And third, it was team work. Bezalel didn't

"We may not be asked to accomplish such a public task as leading a nation out of bondage or creating a place of worship for generations, but God will ask us to fulfill His purposes for our lives. God wants our lives to be something as beautiful and useful to Him as the tabernacle standing among the people in the wilderness."

create the ideas; he began his commission with the designs and specifications God had given Moses. He also received as part of his commission the basic materials he would need for the project (see again the list in 35:4–9). Bezalel was also offered the special skills of others whom he would direct in the creation of a masterpiece suitable to honor God. Bezalel was personally gifted by God for his commission and then equipped and resourced by God for the work he was called to do.

Bezalel executed God's designs in such a way that he met both the letter and the spirit of the commission. There are curtains and then there are curtains, frames and frames, lampstand cups and lampstand cups. Everything that Bezalel made for the tabernacle was useful and beautiful. It was lovely to look at, whether or not it was being used. Little creative details like the lampstand oil cups made in the shape of almond flowers (37:19) speak to the thought and care that went into every detail of the tabernacle. One of the greatest demonstrations of craftsmanship comes from those who can produce a "common" object that is lovely to look at because of its lines and quality and also a delight to use because it is skillfully suited for the task it is designed to carry out.

Bezalel had a team. Oholiab was his right-hand man. But there were many other men and women who contributed their individual abilities to the making of the tabernacle and its furnishings. The phrase "he made" that appears so prominently in these chapters really means that many of these items were created under Bezalel's guidance and direction. He didn't do all the hands-on work, but the final product was a tribute to the special filling God gave him for the great task God asked him to do.

Bezalel was an example of the way God usually works. He doesn't ask us to do things He hasn't equipped us to do or that He will not help us to do. We may not be asked to accomplish such a public task as leading a nation out of bondage or creating a place of worship for generations, but He will ask us to fulfill His purposes for our lives. This adventure begins when we trust in Jesus Christ and receive His gift of the indwelling Holy Spirit. He gifts us as surely as He gifted Bezalel, and His Word is filled with the designs He wants us to carry out in life. We can be Christians who settle for exact obedience to God, or we can be followers of Jesus who pursue creatively exact lives under His grace (see Go Deeper). God wants our lives to be something as beautiful and useful to Him as the tabernacle standing among the people in the wilderness.

Express It

You are a living tabernacle (see Go Deeper). If you have trusted Christ as your Savior, you are filled with the Spirit who gifts you (Rom. 12:6–8) and empowers you (Rom. 15:13) to fulfill that which God has called you to do. Unlike Bezalel, however, who simply was empowered by the Spirit to accomplish a task, the Holy Spirit actually dwells in you (Rom. 8:9). Perhaps this would be a good time to rededicate your tabernacle for its ultimate purpose: to serve as God's dwelling place.

Consider It

As you read Exodus 35:1–37:29, consider these questions:

1) What have been some of the most moving examples of artistic excellence you've seen or experienced in life?

2) How do those experiences help you understand Bezalel's work?

3) What personal qualities was God looking for in those who made contributions for the construction of the tabernacle?

4) What individual skills are noted in these chapters that Bezalel and Oholiab were able to guide in the project?

5) How do we know that an attitude of real generosity filled the camp of Israel during the tabernacle effort?

6) What specific examples of creative exactness can you find in the description of the making of the Ark, the table, the lampstand, and the altar of incense (37:1–29)?

7) When you think of creative exactness in the Christian life, what examples come to mind? (See Go Deeper.)

Worship Workshop

Compared to something as intricate as the human body, the tabernacle was a simple but effective structure. Compared to the massive pyramids and temples the slaves had built in Egypt, the tabernacle barely touched the sands of the wilderness. Yet God chose a simple and movable tent in which to display His glory.

Read Exodus 38:1–39:43

Exodus 38:1–31

Making the Altar of Burnt Offering

38 He made the altar of burnt offering of acacia wood. Five cubits was its length, and five cubits its breadth. It was square, and three cubits was its height. ²He made horns for it on its four corners. Its horns were of one piece with it, and he overlaid it with bronze. ³And he made all the utensils of the altar, the pots, the shovels, the basins, the forks, and the fire pans. He made all its utensils of bronze. ⁴And he made for the altar a grating, a network of bronze, under its ledge, extending halfway down. ⁵He cast four rings on the four corners of the bronze grating as holders for the poles. ⁶He made the poles of acacia wood and overlaid them with bronze. ⁷And he put the poles through the rings on the sides of the altar to carry it with them. He made it hollow, with boards.

Making the Bronze Basin

⁸He made the basin of bronze and its stand of bronze, from the mirrors of the ministering women who ministered in the entrance of the tent of meeting.

Making the Court

⁹And he made the court. For the south side the hangings of the court were of fine twined linen, a hundred cubits; ¹⁰their twenty pillars and their twenty bases were of bronze, but the hooks of the pillars and their fillets were of silver. ¹¹And for the north side there were hangings of a hundred cubits, their twenty pillars, their twenty bases were of bronze, but the hooks of the pillars and their fillets were of silver. ¹²And for the west side were hangings of fifty cubits, their ten pillars, and their ten bases; the hooks of the pillars and their fillets were of silver. ¹³And for the front to the east, fifty cubits. ¹⁴The hangings for one side of the gate were fifteen cubits, with their three pillars and three bases. ¹⁵And

---

> # Key Verse
>
> *Moses saw all the work, and behold, they had done it; as the L*ORD *had commanded, so had they done it. Then Moses blessed them* (Ex. 39:43).

---

so for the other side. On both sides of the gate of the court were hangings of fifteen cubits, with their three pillars and their three bases. ¹⁶All the hangings around the court were of fine twined linen. ¹⁷And the bases for the pillars were of bronze, but the hooks of the pillars and their fillets were of silver. The overlaying of their capitals was also of silver, and all the pillars of the court were filleted with silver. ¹⁸And the screen for the gate of the court was embroidered with needlework in blue and purple and scarlet yarns and fine twined linen. It was twenty cubits long and five cubits high in its breadth, corresponding to the hangings of the court. ¹⁹And their pillars were four in number. Their four bases were of bronze, their hooks of silver, and the overlaying of their capitals and their fillets of silver. ²⁰And all the pegs for the tabernacle and for the court all around were of bronze.

Materials for the Tabernacle

²¹These are the records of the tabernacle, the tabernacle of the testimony, as they were recorded at the commandment of Moses, the responsibility of the Levites under the direction of Ithamar the son of Aaron the priest. ²²Bezalel the son of Uri, son of Hur, of the tribe of Judah, made all that the L*ORD* commanded Moses; ²³and with him was Oholiab the son of Ahisamach,

of the tribe of Dan, an engraver and designer and embroiderer in blue and purple and scarlet yarns and fine twined linen.

²⁴All the gold that was used for the work, in all the construction of the sanctuary, the gold from the offering, was twenty-nine talents and 730 shekels, by the shekel of the sanctuary. ²⁵The silver from those of the congregation who were recorded was a hundred talents and 1,775 shekels, by the shekel of the sanctuary: ²⁶a beka a head (that is, half a shekel, by the shekel of the sanctuary), for everyone who was listed in the records, from twenty years old and upward, for 603,550 men. ²⁷The hundred talents of silver were for casting the bases of the sanctuary and the bases of the veil; a hundred bases for the hundred talents, a talent a base. ²⁸And of the 1,775 shekels he made hooks for the pillars and overlaid their capitals and made fillets for them. ²⁹The bronze that was offered was seventy talents and 2,400 shekels; ³⁰with it he made the bases for the entrance of the tent of meeting, the bronze altar and the bronze grating for it and all the utensils of the altar, ³¹the bases around the court, and the bases of the gate of the court, all the pegs of the tabernacle, and all the pegs around the court.

Go Deeper

It's easy to skim over chapters 36 to 39 in Exodus, noting the repetitive details but finding it hard to visualize the work or the experiences of the workers during those days. The details may even bore us, particularly if we're not artistically minded. But these chapters present us with a challenge to think about the way we approach worship. Is worship just something we do at a certain place during a certain time? Is worship ultimately those all-too-brief moments when we are entirely focused on God, or does worship describe how we go about living each day and doing everything that we do for the glory of God?

It's easy for us to compartmentalize worship into a building rather than letting our awareness of God and our desire to serve and honor Him fill every nook and cranny of our lives. Note how the apostle Paul challenged us to think about worship: "And whatever you do, in word or deed, do everything in the name of the Lord Jesus, giving thanks to God the Father through him" (Col. 3:17). What changes would have to occur in order for you to declare your life a worship workshop? Or to put it another way, how much of your life—habits, work, free time, entertainment—have nothing to do with worship? Do some of those areas need to be altered so that every part of your life allows you places to learn, express, and carry out the worship of your Creator?

Exodus 38 and 39 continue the checklist for the tabernacle that was carefully followed by Moses, Ithamar (Aaron's son), Bezalel, and Oholiab (Ex. 38:21–23). They were clearly an effective task-force. They not only accomplished their assignment, but they also provided a careful accounting of all the resources they used in the project.

We know from Jethro's wise father-in-law counsel (Ex. 18) that Moses did not naturally delegate duties. He was a hands-on leader, which had the advantage of making him a good example but the disadvantage of limiting his effectiveness. Before Jethro came along, Moses was assisted by Aaron, who had been given the position by God. Others, like Joshua, were likely following their natural abilities as leaders and coming alongside Moses without being asked officially. So, Moses' partnership with Ithamar, Bezalel, and Oholiab was surely a significant learning experience for him. A lot was at stake. God had already been offended by the people's blatant disregard for His commandments. It may have been difficult for Moses to entrust so much responsibility to others. But there was only so much he could do.

Since these records were probably originally Moses' journals, there are some interesting little details that indicate Moses may have been amazed by the skill and ingenuity of those who were doing the actual artistic work on the tabernacle and the priests' clothing. Exodus 38:8 notes that Bezalel "made the basin of bronze" from the "mirrors of the ministering women." This gives us an idea of one group's generosity in giving what would have been prized possessions for use in creating the tabernacle's furnishings. Exodus 39:3 reveals the process of creating the gold thread that was woven into the fabric of the priests' clothing. That kind of detailed description sounds like it comes from someone who observed with open-mouthed appreciation the skill of those who created sheets of delicate hammered gold foil and then painstakingly cut them into threads. Moses must have been speechless.

The phrase "as the LORD had commanded Moses" that appears repeatedly in this section (39:1, 5, 7, 21, 26, 29, 31, 42), should probably be read with a sigh of relief. God had given the command,

"Moses would have reminded them that all their careful work was actually worship. They were doing it unto the Lord. God was being honored, valued, and treated as worthy by those who painstakingly carried out their assignments in the creation of the tabernacle."

Moses had received it, but others faithfully carried it out with meticulous care. Note how chapter 39 ends with a host of the people approaching Moses: "Then they brought the tabernacle to Moses, the tent and all its utensils, its hooks, its frames, its bars, its pillars, and its bases" (39:33). The "packing list" goes on and on. Imagine the scene as artist after artist delivered to Bezalel, Oholiab, and Moses their carefully stacked or folded masterpieces. The larger items would have been presented by groups who had labored day and night to create their assignments for God's magnificent commission. Everything would have been placed in a certain order, since the expectation was that the entire tabernacle would be erected almost immediately.

Moses stood looking at the results of Spirit-motivated work. His description of the moment is subdued in Exodus but must have been emotion-packed when it was carried out live. It appears that he may have whispered over and over during the presentation, "You did it!" Here is his report: "And Moses saw all the work, and behold, they had done it; as the Lord had commanded, so had they done it. Then Moses blessed them" (39:43). We would miss a blessing ourselves if we read that last phrase as if Moses responded to the people's effort with "Well, bless you!"

The word *blessing* describes; it doesn't specify. But a blessing involves saying and delivering good into another person's life. Moses would have reminded them that all their careful work was actually worship. They were doing it unto the Lord. God was being honored, valued, and treated as worthy by those who painstakingly carried out their assignments in the creation of the tabernacle. The weeks during which the entire nation had focused on God's commission had turned the nation into a worship workshop. Everyone was involved. Probably everyone helped in some way—through giving, sewing, building, casting, hammering, shaping, as well as those caring for the people who were doing the actual hands-on work. For those weeks, Israel was living for God. In blessing them, Moses would have pointed out what God had been doing in them as they worked and what He would continue to do for them and in them as they worshiped and obeyed God in the future.

Express It

As you pray, ask God to help you develop a clear picture of the life-commission He has for you. Ask Him for vision to see what He wants you to present as finished to Him when your life is over. If you long to hear Him say, "Well done, good and faithful servant," how often are you asking Him, "Lord what is it that You want me to 'well-do'? Where can I be more faithful as Your servant?"

Consider It

As you read Exodus 38:1–39:43, consider these questions:

1) What item among all the furnishings for the tabernacle do you think you would have enjoyed working on?

2) Why do you think the taskforce's report on the work was so detailed?

3) How many parts of your life right now do you think of as part of your commission from God to carry out faithfully?

4) What parts of your commission have been satisfying?

5) How do you think you will feel about eventually presenting your life to God, even as the craftsmen and women brought all the finished tabernacle work to Moses?

6) In what ways have you been blessed by God and others as you have carried out your assignments in life for God?

7) What other observations do you think could be made about Moses' state of mind and heart during those busy days?

God's Exit Strategy

God can certainly do things quickly. But He is never in a hurry. He always works by His timetable, and His purposes always get accomplished. The time it took to free Israel from bondage in Egypt was exactly the right amount of time. God accomplished His exit strategy.

Read Exodus 40:1–38

The Tabernacle Erected

40 The LORD spoke to Moses, saying, ²"On the first day of the first month you shall erect the tabernacle of the tent of meeting. ³And you shall put in it the ark of the testimony, and you shall screen the ark with the veil. ⁴And you shall bring in the table and arrange it, and you shall bring in the lampstand and set up its lamps. ⁵And you shall put the golden altar for incense before the ark of the testimony, and set up the screen for the door of the tabernacle. ⁶You shall set the altar of burnt offering before the door of the tabernacle of the tent of meeting, ⁷and place the basin between the tent of meeting and the altar, and put water in it. ⁸And you shall set up the court all around, and hang up the screen for the gate of the court.

⁹"Then you shall take the anointing oil and anoint the tabernacle and all that is in it, and consecrate it and all its furniture, so that it may become holy. ¹⁰You shall also anoint the altar of burnt offering and all its utensils, and consecrate the altar, so that the altar may become most holy. ¹¹You shall also anoint the basin and its stand, and consecrate it. ¹²Then you shall bring Aaron and his sons to the entrance of the tent of meeting and shall wash them with water ¹³and put on Aaron the holy garments. And you shall anoint him and consecrate him, that he may serve me as priest. ¹⁴You shall bring his sons also and put coats on them, ¹⁵and anoint them, as you anointed their father, that they may serve me as priests. And their anointing shall admit them to a perpetual priesthood throughout their generations."

¹⁶This Moses did; according to all that the LORD commanded him, so he did. ¹⁷In the first month in the second year, on the first day of the month, the tabernacle was erected. ¹⁸Moses erected the

> # Key Verse
>
> *For the cloud of the LORD was on the tabernacle by day, and fire was in it by night, in the sight of all the house of Israel throughout all their journeys* (Ex. 40:38).

tabernacle. He laid its bases, and set up its frames, and put in its poles, and raised up its pillars. ¹⁹And he spread the tent over the tabernacle and put the covering of the tent over it, as the LORD had commanded Moses. ²⁰He took the testimony and put it into the ark, and put the poles on the ark and set the mercy seat above on the ark. ²¹And he brought the ark into the tabernacle and set up the veil of the screen, and screened the ark of the testimony, as the LORD had commanded Moses. ²²He put the table in the tent of meeting, on the north side of the tabernacle, outside the veil, ²³and arranged the bread on it before the LORD, as the LORD had commanded Moses. ²⁴He put the lampstand in the tent of meeting, opposite the table on the south side of the tabernacle, ²⁵and set up the lamps before the LORD, as the LORD had commanded Moses. ²⁶He put the golden altar in the tent of meeting before the veil, ²⁷and burned fragrant incense on it, as the LORD had commanded Moses. ²⁸He put in place the screen for the door of the tabernacle. ²⁹And he set the altar of burnt offering at the entrance of the tabernacle of the tent of meeting, and offered on it the burnt offering and the grain offering, as the LORD had commanded Moses. ³⁰He set the basin between the tent of meeting and the altar, and put water in it for washing, ³¹with which Moses and Aaron and his sons washed their hands and their feet. ³²When they went into the tent of meeting, and when they approached the altar, they washed, as the Lord commanded Moses. ³³And he erected the court around the tabernacle and the altar, and set up the screen of the gate of the court. So Moses finished the work.

The Glory of the Lord

³⁴Then the cloud covered the tent of meeting, and the glory of the Lord filled the tabernacle. ³⁵And Moses was not able to enter the tent of meeting because the cloud settled on it, and the glory of the Lord filled the tabernacle. ³⁶Throughout all their journeys, whenever the cloud was taken up from over the tabernacle, the people of Israel would set out. ³⁷But if the cloud was not taken up, then they did not set out till the day that it was taken up. ³⁸For the cloud of the Lord was on the tabernacle by day, and fire was in it by night, in the sight of all the house of Israel throughout all their journeys.

Go Deeper

Exodus 40:34 tells us that "the glory of the Lord filled the tabernacle." As if to make the point of this remarkable event, verse 35 reports that even Moses "was not able to enter the tent of meeting because the cloud settled on it, and the glory of the Lord filled the tabernacle." There is probably no greater word for God's undeniable and overwhelming presence than the word "glory." In Hebrew, one of the ideas connected to the word is weight, as in seriousness, significance, and impact. When there is even a hint of God's glory somewhere, everything else fades into secondary position.

Take a few minutes to survey God's glory throughout Exodus. It is specifically mentioned in Exodus 16:7, 10; 24:16, 17; 29:43; 33:18, 22; 40:34, 35. Notice the related terms in Exodus 15:1, 6, 11, and 21. Moses was exposed to God's glory in a unique way (Ex. 33:18–22). As a result, his face was changed in appearance (Ex. 34:29–35). Consider how your attitudes and appearance are changed by the time you spend with God. Do people ever see His glory in you, or is there always too much of you for people to see God's glory?

God took a few months to get Israel out of Egypt. God took 40 years to get Egypt out of Israel. When God heard Israel cry out at the beginning of Exodus, the Israelites were making bricks and building cities for Pharaoh. At the end of Exodus, Israel had left Egypt, and the people were gathered around an awe-inspiring tabernacle they had constructed for the Lord, watching as God's glory filled and overflowed the special place He had designed.

God took 80 years to prepare His servant Moses for a 40-year job. God's exit strategy for His people required the development of a suitable leader. As always, God's training in someone's life, even someone like Moses, is a work in progress. And Exodus only covers the early phases of Moses' work as Israel's leader. The real wilderness wanderings had not yet started. Exodus 40 records the first assembling of the tabernacle, which occurred approximately one year after the departure from Egypt.

Moses is one of the few people in the Bible whose life we can trace from start to finish. Exodus records his birth; Deuteronomy records his death. God's work in Moses throughout his life offers us many lessons that can be applied to God's work in our lives. For example, God never needs to get to know us better; He knows us intuitively, through and through. But we don't know ourselves very well, and God's work in us helps us discover who we are as well as who He is! We get to see in great detail in Moses' life, and to a lesser detail in the lives of his peers, the way God brings people along. Moses' experiences invite us to ask, "How well am I responding to God's work in my life?"

Exodus fills an important role in the Pentateuch (the first five books of the Bible). Genesis covers more time and history than any other book in the Bible. It takes us from the creation of everything to God's choosing a family through which He will build a people called Israel. Exodus then gives us a documentary-style report of the tumultuous months surrounding Israel's birth as a nation. Leviticus and Numbers fill in the background details, record the tragedy of the nation's refusal to enter the Promised Land, and provide an itinerary of the wanderings. Deuteronomy represents Moses' public review

> *"God never needs to get to know us better; He knows us intuitively, through and through. But we don't know ourselves very well, and God's work in us helps us discover who we are as well as who He is!"*

and final message to the people he led for over 40 years. Along the way, Moses discovered that even he was not exempt from having to obey God's orders. He led the people out of Egypt, but he was not permitted to lead them into the Promised Land. Of all the adults who followed Moses out of Egypt, only two (Joshua and Caleb) survived the wilderness wanderings. With those two exceptions, everyone who eventually entered the Promised Land was under age 20 when they left Egypt or was born in the desert.

Exodus 40 brings us to the end of the beginning. A year after leaving Egypt, Israel was ready to begin its life as a nation. God had provided them with freedom and given them directions for an orderly life together. God had directed them to create a structure that would serve to remind them of His unique presence among them as a nation. All the parts and pieces of the tabernacle were assembled before Moses (Ex. 39). God then gave the command for the first erecting of the tabernacle. Again, though Moses was doing this work, the Levites were actually charged with the hands-on delegation of fitting pole A into curtain D and hook Y. Eventually, this task would became routine; the first time, things must have gone slowly and carefully, with a lot of direction from Moses, Bezalel, and Oholiab. The Levites put the tabernacle together as several million other Israelites looked on in expectation. What would happen next?

God Himself consecrated the finished tabernacle. He covered and filled it with His cloud and the pillar of fire. God's presence became the daily signal to the people. When the cloud stayed in place, so did they. When it moved, so did the people. Exodus began with a bush on fire that wasn't consumed; it ends with a tabernacle on godly fire every night but not consumed. Along with the Israelites, we worship an awesome God.

Express It

As you pray, express your appreciation to God for the lessons you have learned in Exodus. Ask God to show you parallels in your life to the experiences of the Israelites leaving Egypt. If you are a follower of Jesus, He has freed you from bondage to sin. Are you making steady headway toward the eternal Promised Land that God has given you freely in Christ or are you wandering in a desert—still trying to find your own way home or find acceptance with God? Thank God for His immeasurable gift in Christ!

Consider It

As you read Exodus 40:1–38, consider these questions:

1) What lasting new insights have you gained from this journey through Exodus?

_____

_____

2) What aspect of God's character do you find most striking as it is revealed in this particular Old Testament book?

_____

_____

3) When you think about Moses' character and experiences, what stands out the most for you about this man of God?

_____

_____

4) How does chapter 40 provide a good stopping place for this particular extended episode in the life of Israel?

_____

_____

5) Do you think anyone wondered why they were taking so much time and effort to build a sturdy movable tabernacle when, at that point, they only expected to be in the wilderness a few more weeks? Why or why not?

_____

_____

6) What moments in your life have paralleled that occasion when Moses first oversaw the erecting of the tabernacle? When has "everything come together" like that in your life?

_____

_____

7) How has this study of Exodus affected your relationship with God?

_____

_____

Notes

Notes

Notes

Notes

Notes

Notes

Notes

Notes

Notes

Notes